CASE∗METHOD^{SM}

Entity Relationship Modelling

About the Author

Richard Barker was born in Sheffield, England, in 1946. He went to Edinburgh University where he studied Chemistry, but realized that his interests lay outside the realms of pure science.

He has gained insight into many aspects of information systems through work in manufacturing industry and the Health Service, and the early introduction of database and data dictionary software whilst working with a major hardware company. Subsequently, Richard led a consultancy team specializing in strategic analysis and systems development using structured methods.

He is currently a main board director of ORACLE Corporation UK Limited, and a Senior Vice President of ORACLE Europe, responsible for the Oracle system development method, CASE*Method, and the development of Computer-Aided Systems Engineering (CASE) and Application Package software using the ORACLE RDBMS. He established the UK Training Division to provide education for clients and Oracle staff alike in the use of Oracle products, methods and strategic thinking, and has lectured widely on network and relational database technology, distributed databases, CASE and user involvement in systems development.

Richard is married with three children, and lives in Berkshire, England.

CASE*METHOD^{SM}

Entity Relationship Modelling

RICHARD BARKER

An imprint of Pearson Education

Harlow, England · London · New York · Reading, Massachusetts · San Francisco · Toronto · Don Mills, Ontario · Sydney
Tokyo · Singapore · Hong Kong · Seoul · Taipei · Cape Town · Madrid · Mexico City · Amsterdam · Munich · Paris · Milan

The Relational Database Management System

PEARSON EDUCATION LIMITED

Head Office:
Edinburgh Gate
Harlow CM20 2JE
England
Tel: +44 (0)1279 623623
Fax: +44 (0)1279 431059

London Office:
128 Long Acre
London WC2E 9AN
Tel: +44 (0)207 477 2000
Fax: +44 (0)207 240 5771

Website: *www.awl-he.com/computing*
www. awl.com/cseng

First published in Great Britain 1989

ISBN 0-201-41696-4

The programs in this book have been included for their instructional value. The publisher does not offer any warranties or representation in respect of their fitness for a particular purpose, nor does the publisher accept any liability for any loss or damage arising from their use.

Many of the designations used by manufacturers and sellers to distinguish their products are claimed as trademarks. Addison-Wesley has made every attempt to supply trademark information about manufacturers and their products mentioned in this book. CASE*Method, CASE* Dictionary and CASE*Designers are trademarks of Oracle Corporation. Merise is a method recommended by the French Government. SSADM is a method recommended by the UK Government. IEM is a proprietary method from James Martin Associates in association with Texas Instruments. Chen is a proprietary method from Chen Associates.

20 19 18 17 16 15

Edited and illustrated by Barbara Barker.
Cover design by Hybert Design & Type, Maidenhead.
Printed and bound in the United States of America

The Publishers' policy is to use paper manufactured from sustainable forests.

FOREWORD

Information should be viewed not only as a valuable corporate asset but also as the starting point for building a corporate information system. As a matter of fact, many organizations are finding that understanding what corporate information is needed is a necessary prerequisite for building high-quality, well-integrated information systems. For this reason, a major and important software technology trend for MIS departments is to move from procedure-oriented to data-oriented application development methods. Information engineering is becoming the most popular data-oriented, full life-cycle development methodology.

Information engineering is often described as an information-centered development approach. It is an overall system development strategy that focuses on strategic information planning and understanding the business goals. It is built on the basic premise that corporate information systems can be better integrated if the data that they share are controlled centrally by being part of the same logical data model.

Information engineering advocates looking across all information systems in a corporation to identify how information is used and shared. Program structures then are "built on top of" an enterprise-wide data model that establishes a common information infrastructure for writing the information systems used throughout a corporation. Thus, procedures follow from data, and the quality of the information systems depends upon the quality of the data model.

Discovering what information is used in an organization is a difficult, time-consuming task. Experienced analysts aided by powerful tools and proper techniques can help ensure that corporate information is accurately and consistently defined.

Entity relationship modelling is an information engineering technique used to develop a high-quality data model. The data model provides a standard way of defining data and the relationships among data for all information systems. This greatly improves system quality and increases software productivity.

Entity relationship modelling is becoming the universal technique for data modelling. As such, every business systems analyst needs to learn and use entity relationship modelling. To date there are few courses and texts that teach this technique. This book was written by Richard Barker, an experienced analyst who has evolved and applied the technique in hundreds of projects over the last twenty years. In the book, Mr Barker introduces entity relationship modelling along with its underlying terminology and suggested guidelines. He uses real-world examples - first simple and then more complex - which is the easiest way to learn a new method. He also explains how entity relationship modelling can be supported with CASE tools. Once entity-relationship modelling is mastered, this book can be used as a reference book since its appendices summarize the basic concepts and terminology.

Carma McClure
September 1989

PREFACE

Purpose

The purpose of this book is to provide data analysts, strategists and data administrators with a definitive guide to Entity Relationship Modelling. At the same time, I was very keen that the book should be well-thumbed by regular use, as opposed to sitting on someone's shelf.

I believe that a sound grasp of entity relationship modelling can provide a firm architectural framework for understanding a business and creating flexible systems for the future. There are, however, many things that need to be considered over a period of time to take advantage of these basic techniques.

Not least of these considerations is understanding the meaning of words as applied by our users and separately within the Information Systems department. It is certainly my experience that many system developments fail because of the use of jargon and protectionism within the ivory tower of the Information Systems department, coupled with the bewildering explosion of technology. In this book I am implicitly recommending that analysts must discard their egos, and instead recognize that there is strength in their human fallibility. In practical terms it means seeking out the most thorough and accurate understanding of the business, and then exposing that to your users and peers so they can help you gain even more accuracy. I have seen this 'egoless' team approach not only enable teams to build far more appropriate systems but act as a catalyst, knitting together users, system development staff and even accountants.

How to Use This Book

I hope this book will be used by novice and expert alike. It has, therefore, been designed to provide easy-reading, tutorial-like chapters (marked ▭) and definitive reference chapters and appendices (marked ■). Later chapters contain more complex examples and techniques to be used once you have mastered the basic techniques. A single example runs through the book, based on a hypothetical airline. However, other examples and common problems are provided to help minimize your learning curve.

The appendices are designed to cover other useful concepts, further detail quality checks, first-cut database design and data administration. All the important terms in the book are covered by the glossary and, finally, an extensive index and the contents list are there to provide alternative entry points to the information in the book.

This book should provide 'hot-line' support to your entity relationship modelling when that really key problem requires urgent resolution.

Acknowledgements

Writing a book about something you have been doing for years sounds straightforward. I found myself going over projects and discussions from the last twenty years. It is really amazing what I have learnt from my colleagues in England and the United States, and especially from many of the users who kept insisting that we really must cater for yet another important exception.

Ensuring that the book itself is complete, consistent and coherent was a tedious but worthwhile task. I would like to thank my close colleagues who took the time to expose ambiguities, difficulty in understanding, errors and omissions. In particular I would like to say a special thank you to Barbara, my wife, with whom I have worked weekends and into the early hours whilst we struggled with definitions, style, diagrams and terminology.

Richard Barker
July, 1989

CONTENTS

Appendices

Chapter

1

INTRODUCTION

Entity Relationship Modelling is a technique for defining the information needs of your organization. It provides a firm foundation for delivering high-quality, appropriate systems that meet your business needs. Other techniques, such as function modelling and the use of interviewing techniques, are covered by other books in this series.

In its simplest form, Entity Relationship Modelling involves identifying the things of importance in an organization (**entities**), the properties of those things (**attributes**) and how they are related to one another (**relationships**). But this is only of value within the context of what is done in the business and how these business functions act upon this information model.

Objectives of Entity Relationship Modelling

To provide an accurate model of the information needs of the organization, which will act as a framework for development of new or enhanced systems.

To provide a model independent of any data storage and access method, to allow objective decisions to be made about implementation techniques and coexistence with existing systems.

Generic Models

Modelling has always been accepted by engineers, scientists, artists and accountants as an invaluable technique for presenting ideas, aiding understanding and giving insight, and even predicting new ways of doing things. Indeed, scientific theories are models not hard facts, designed on the basis of the evidence available at the time they are put forward. Many models are refined in the light of further evidence and some are finally discarded when their limitations are discovered.

Arguably our own perception of the world is an elaborate model we create in our brains from the information we have gathered. We then hold it in such a way that it can be used to help us explain and cope with novel situations. Our imaginations and creative thinking make full use of our intellectual model of the world.

Good modelling techniques are supported by rigorous standards and conventions to remove ambiguity and aid communication. Entity relationship modelling is just such a technique, which is applicable to the information needs of any organization in any industry.

Why is Entity Relationship Modelling Important?

During the past twenty years, computer systems have become more and more sophisticated. They have matured through many evolutions:

- experimentation
- isolated functional systems
- departmental systems
- integrated operational systems
- office automation
- management information.

As this progression occurred, only lip-service was paid to minimizing duplications and ensuring true integration of data, the integrity of data and real availability of information. This was partly because the scope of systems was nearly always limited, and the idea of being able to understand the diverse and often conflicting needs of different users was beyond the vision, skill, experience and tools that could be applied.

Modern entity relationship modelling, in association with sophisticated CASE tools, can provide an effective and timely means of defining and controlling the definition of your information needs. But this technique and supporting CASE tools **must** be used in the correct manner, just like any other powerful tool.

This book gives guidance on how to create, validate and exploit entity relationship modelling to help you build good computer and/or manual systems. These techniques have been used for over twenty years in many diverse circumstances to provide solutions implemented on relational, network, hierarchic and conventional computer systems and to aid the design of paper forms, filing and control procedures.

It is recommended that you use the book in association with a good course on the subject, ideally combined with a period of work alongside an experienced modeller.

There is no substitute for experience.

**Figure 1-1
The Business System
Life Cycle**

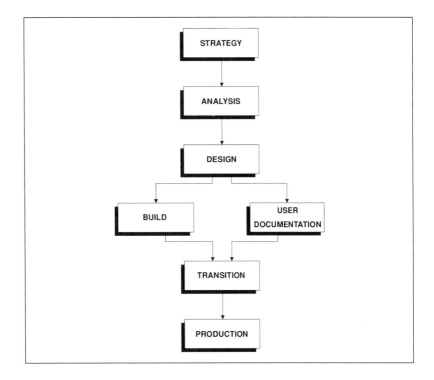

**Applicability to the
Business System Life Cycle**

The techniques covered by this book apply in particular to the Strategy and Analysis stages of the Business System Life Cycle. The principles, however, are also applicable during database design and when change is being considered during production. The life-cycle is covered in detail in the publication entitled *CASE*Method – Tasks and Deliverables*.

Your Challenge

The systems being demanded for today and for the future are expected to provide simultaneous support for the various needs of any organization – for day-to-day operations, for management information and for other requirements at local, central and decentralized levels. These systems must also encompass the many alternative methods of implementation available, ranging from simple manual files and office systems through to the sophistication of heterogeneous distributed databases. Contemplating creating such systems without the understanding and rigour to be gained by using modelling techniques is hardly conceivable.

Ten Key Issues

There are ten key issues that need to be considered when using entity relationship modelling to help you define the information needs of your business.

Figure 1-2
Ten Key Issues

Key Issues

- Data, a Key Resource
- Management Commitment
- Conventions
- Minimum Definition
- Data Independence
- Generic Patterns
- Attitude and Quality
- Communication
- Relevance
- A Means, Not an End

Data, a Key Resource

Data, as a resource, is nowadays accepted as being as important to the successful running of an organization as are financial, human and physical resources. Progressive companies often gain much of their competitive edge by the control of this vital information resource.

Management Commitment

Management time must be gained to confirm the requirements for information. No matter how talented you are at modelling, you will have limited success without the commitment of the managers.

Conventions

Rigorous conventions, standards and guidelines must be applied at all times, including the concepts of data normalization.

Minimum Definition

Any information or data concept should be defined and modelled in one and only one way, and then associations set up to all its related objects. For example, a thing called a 'Purchase Order' should be defined once and then related to department, products, authorization functions, and so on, as required; that is, true database principles applied to these modelling techniques.

Data Independence

Information requirements must be defined in a manner that is independent of any eventual storage or access method to enable a creative and objective view to be taken of the business and subsequent design. (See Figure 1-3.)

Figure 1-3
Different Methods for
Handling Data

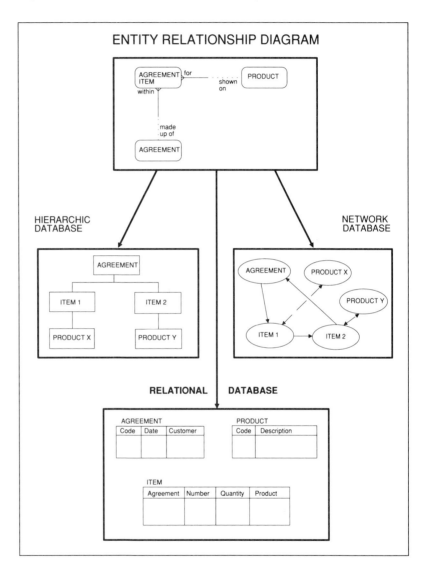

Generic Patterns

Recurring patterns of data should be sought to enable the users in your business to exploit this opportunity to streamline how their data could be processed, and to suggest more cost-effective and flexible structures to the database designers.

Attitude and Quality

Modellers must learn to apply the conventions automatically and with speed, but without sacrificing rigour. They must also take every opportunity with their users and peers to improve the accuracy of their models.

An objective is to understand 100% of the information needs of the organization so that systems can be built which support 82% of these needs.

This is the normal 80:20 rule, but with the addition of that extra few percent that pre-empts problems and encourages more generic and flexible designs. Thus, maintenance costs can be decreased by a very large factor.

Communication

Communication with end users must be in terms that they can understand and yet it must remain rigorous. These modelling techniques have been used for many years to help top executives, directors, managers and others understand their business. It is essential to use clear English, no abbreviations and no jargon, to achieve this understanding. For example, it is recommended that you do not even use the word entity with an end user!

Always talk in terms of the **actual** things of significance ('about which information needs to be known or held'). It is helpful to use examples with direct relevance to the end user. Whilst this may seem patently obvious, we all tend to have our own favourite examples, precisely because they have a special relevance to us. But to use a situation that occurred in a company supplying sporting goods may not be an appropriate example for an international airline!

Relevance

Information requirements can only be of value if they support the functional needs of the organization, within the framework of the business objectives and aims.

A Means, Not an End

Whilst entity relationship modelling is very powerful, giving incredible insight into a company and acting as a framework for data design, it is only an intermediate technique, albeit an important one.

Chapter

2   A SIMPLE EXAMPLE

Before we get into the full theory and rigour of entity relationship modelling, let us take an example from a hypothetical company and see how it may be modelled. Given that overview, we will then have a quick look at how that model could be implemented.

The concepts used in this chapter are defined in detail in Chapter 3 and definitions are given in the Glossary.

The Example –
Tickets for Airlines

When travelling by air on a standard airline, a very tangible concept is the ticket, which might cover a journey from say Atlantia, the capital city of the island group Atlantis, to Paris. If you look carefully you will notice that a ticket is made up of coupons, each of which is for a flight between two airports. Such a ticket for a hypothetical airline called 'Atlantis Island Flights' is shown below.

Figure 2-1
An Airline Ticket

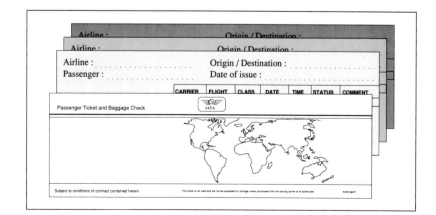

The ticket actually consists of two coupons, one from Atlantia to London and the other from London to Paris. The third sheet is the copy to be retained, which shows the entire journey.

Figure 2-2
An Airline Ticket Coupon

Airline :	Atlantis Island Flights		Origin / Destination :			Atlantia		
Passenger :	R.JONES		Date of issue :			3 May 89		

		CARRIER	FLIGHT	CLASS	DATE	TIME	STATUS	COMMENT
From	Atlantia	AA	AIF	213	N	5/06/89	08.00	OK	
To	London	HR	BA	424	N	6/06/89	21.30	OK	
To	Paris	CD						

Fare :   US$ 845

Let us now look at the same area of information from the perspective of the aircraft.

Each aircraft will typically make several flights each day, identified by the date and time of departure, the flight number and the departure airport. The flight number gives us two pieces of information: the first part tells us the airline – in this case 'AIF' means the Atlantis Island Flights airline. The second part uniquely identifies a route that the airline flies. We therefore need to know which aircraft have been assigned to which flights, how many tickets have been sold, whether the flights have been confirmed and which seats have been allocated.

Figure 2-3
Entity Relationship Model
of the Ticket

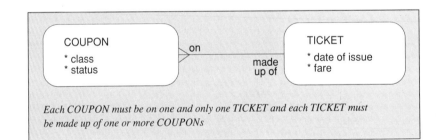

The nucleus of this simple system is the coupon. It is significant as the lowest common denominator and has vital information such as its class and status. It can only exist within the context of a ticket, from which it inherits the date of issue and fare.

Each of the boxes on the diagram in Figure 2-3 is an entity and the line between is a relationship. The line has a forked (many) ending on the left and a single (one) ending on the right, indicating that there can be many coupons on one ticket: a many to one relationship. The line is solid to show that the relationship is mandatory. The relationship can be read from left to right to tell us that:

Each COUPON must be on one and only one TICKET

and reading from right to left:

Each TICKET must be made up of one or more COUPONs.

Notice that the phrase 'must be' is used to tell us that this is a mandatory relationship.

But what about the flight?

Figure 2-4
TICKET to FLIGHT Relationship

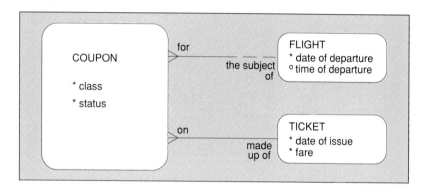

Now we can see that a coupon is in some way related to a flight. The diagram now reads from left to right:

Each COUPON must be for one and only one FLIGHT

and conversely from right to left:

Each FLIGHT may be the subject of one or more COUPONs.

Notice that the flight may not be the subject of any coupons at all! (This is shown by the dotted part of the line, which means the relationship is optional – may be.) This could be because the flight has only just been put into the schedule, or we have not sold any coupons for it yet. In either case, starting at flight and looking along the relationship to coupon gives us some useful information.

We now have a strong relationship between a ticket and flight, via the coupon. In fact, this is a many to many relationship, as is shown below, which reflects the true business situation.

Each TICKET must be made up of one or more COUPONs, each of which is for a (different) FLIGHT, and, conversely, each FLIGHT may be the subject of one or more COUPONs (hopefully a full flight) each of which must be on a (different) TICKET.

Other useful information is shown by the words inside the boxes. These **attributes** provide more detailed description of the entities, which can be read as follows:

Each TICKET has a date of issue and a fare.

A Short Summary

Before moving on, let us have a quick look at what we have found so far about the technique. A box represents an entity, with a name in capitals and attributes shown in lower case. Two entities may be associated by a relationship and we have looked at two many to one relationships, shown by ⟫————— . These relationships may be read out in English, using a special syntax. For now it is useful to note that a solid line along half of the relationship is read as **must be** (mandatory) and a dotted line is read as **may be** (optional). This syntax will be covered in detail in the next chapter.

Let us now extend the model a little further.

Figure 2-5
Core Model

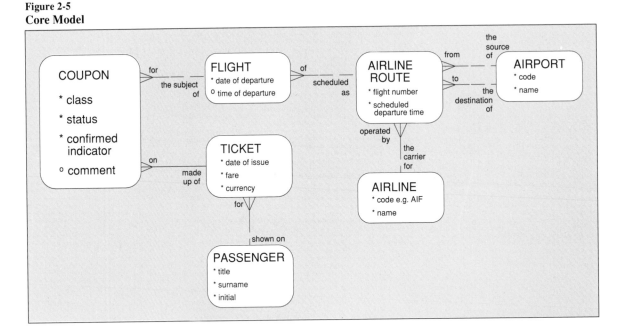

The core model in Figure 2-5 now has enough information on it to model the original ticket. Notice that we now have boxes for each real thing mentioned on the ticket. We have added boxes for passenger, airport, airline and, perhaps the most difficult one to understand, an airline route.

An airline route is uniquely identified by a flight number and its associated airline. This is shown on the ticket by a structured code such as AIF213 or AIF217.

We can now read the diagram from the AIRLINE box as follows:

Each AIRLINE may be the carrier for one or more AIRLINE ROUTEs, each of which may be scheduled as one or more (actual) FLIGHTs, further described by their date and time of departure. According to the diagram, each FLIGHT must be of a (pre-defined) AIRLINE ROUTE (non-standard flights are not yet allowed!) and must be from one AIRPORT to another AIRPORT.

This is a useful and rigorous set of business rules.

The above sentence, which was read from the entity relationship model, could be viewed from two different angles.

Angle 1

Which flights are scheduled at Atlantia Airport from any airline?
This would typically be used for display to departing passengers.

Figure 2-6
Airport Departures

AIRPORT   DEPARTURES

Airport :   Atlantia

Airline	Flight Number	Departure		Destination
		Date	Time	
BA	962	3 Jan 89	07.30	London
AIF	213	3 Jan 89	08.00	London
AIF	004	3 Jan 89	08.15	NewYork
BA	964	3 Jan 89	09.00	Manchester
TW	51	3 Jan 89	09.15	Chicago

Angle 2

What flights has Atlantis Island Flights got scheduled from Atlantia?
This would be used by AIF to keep a track of its own flights.

Figure 2-7
Airline Departures

AIRLINE   DEPARTURES

Airline :   Atlantis Island Flights (AIF)
Airport :   Atlantia

Flight Number	To		Departure	
			Date	Time
213	London	LHR	3 Jan 89	08.00
004	New York	JFK	3 Jan 89	08.15
009	South Island	AASI	3 Jan 89	09.20

In other words, good airlines will have a computer database or manual system that can be used to record, report on and control the information modelled on the Entity Relationship Diagram.

How Did We Get There?

Every time the information on the ticket or coupon referred to some real-world thing we created an entity for it (represented by a box with a name in capitals), and then put the data we were given as attributes of the appropriate thing. (An attribute is any description of an entity.) For example, the entity AIRLINE has an attribute called code. Whenever we found a significant association between two entities, we added a line with words on both ends to represent the relationships.

In the real world the codes and names are often used to represent relationships. For example, on our picture of the coupon on a ticket (see Figure 2-2) the code AIF was used in the column headed carrier to signify some relationship to the Atlantis Island Flights airline. On our diagram, however, this indirect relationship was shown by the lines from COUPON to FLIGHT to AIRLINE ROUTE and thus to AIRLINE, and AIF was merely a value for the attribute of AIRLINE called code.

But the diagram still does not cover the actual aircraft, the confirmation and the seat allocation. The diagram in Figure 2-8 does that.

Figure 2-8
Extended Model

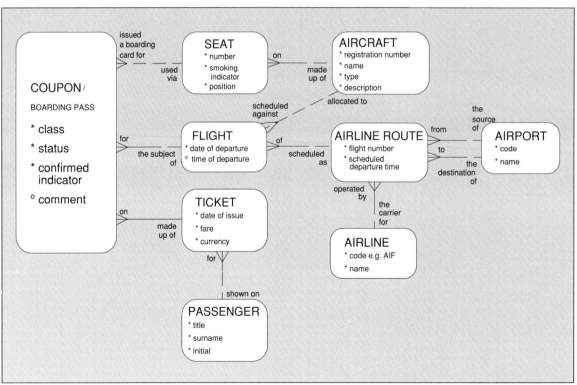

Now we can look at the information from the point of view of the aircraft.

Each AIRCRAFT may be allocated to one or more FLIGHTs with a date and time of departure and

Each FLIGHT must be of a standard AIRLINE ROUTE from an AIRPORT to another AIRPORT.

(The model even allows an airline route from an airport back to itself! This is conceivable when one considers joy-rides for a couple of hours in Concorde.)

To complete the seat allocation we must somehow assign a person to a seat on an aircraft. This is achieved by issuing a boarding pass against the coupon, and for now this is shown as a synonym or alternative name for a coupon, as below.

Each AIRCRAFT may also be made up of one or more SEATS, each of which will hopefully be used via one or more COUPONs (or BOARDING PASSes) for a FLIGHT on a particular departure date and time.

Notice that we have linked the ticket to the passenger and catered for a passenger having more than one ticket over a period of time.

Each TICKET must be for one and only one PASSENGER, who may be shown on one or more TICKETs.

PASSENGER is a useful entity as we may subsequently extend the model to help the airline personalize its service by giving a passenger his or her preferred seat position.

Now any **good** system should ensure that a coupon/boarding pass is unique to a seat for a particular flight, although prior to seat allocation some level of overbooking is standard.

From the coupon/boarding pass we can obviously identify the list of passengers we have on board, which could be very useful in case of emergencies or if a passenger has not yet boarded the aircraft a few minutes before its departure time. We might now look at how the information might appear in a real system, in this case portrayed graphically.

Figure 2-9
Seating Allocation Screen

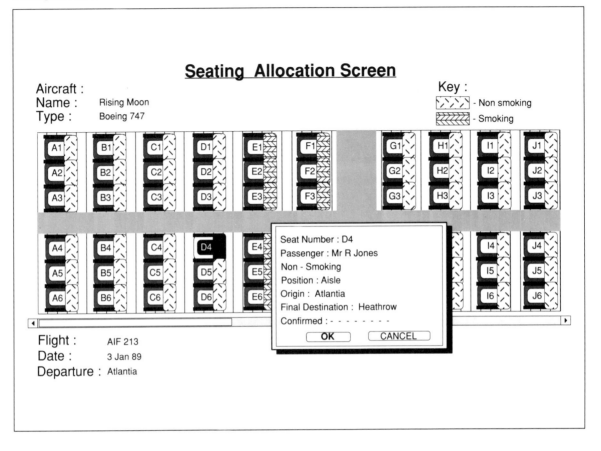

Seating Allocation Screen

Aircraft :
Name :   Rising Moon
Type :   Boeing 747

Key :
- Non smoking
- Smoking

Seat Number : D4
Passenger : Mr R Jones
Non - Smoking
Position : Aisle
Origin : Atlantia
Final Destination : Heathrow
Confirmed : - - - - - - - -

OK   CANCEL

Flight :   AIF 213
Date :   3 Jan 89
Departure : Atlantia

The picture above illustrates a possible current or envisaged implementation of an airline booking system, for use at the booking-in desks. The seating arrangement of the aircraft has been laid out graphically, illustrating the many to one relationship between seat and aircraft. Shading is used to represent the smoking/non-smoking classification, represented on our Entity Relationship Diagram by the **smoking indicator** attribute on the SEAT entity. In this case, seat D4 has been selected by using a mouse as a pointing device; a pop-up window has appeared in which the passenger details are entered or confirmed. When this information is complete, clicking on the OK button on the window will complete the transaction and the booking.

Database Implementation

Let us briefly have a look at how the model for COUPON, SEAT and AIRCRAFT might be organized in different types of database.

Relational Database

With a relational database, each entity would become a table as illustrated below, and the attributes would become columns in the tables.

**Figure 2-10
Relational Design**

Table	Columns			
AIRCRAFT	Name	char(40)	not null	
	Registration number	char(20)	not null	
	Type	char(6)	not null	
	Description	char(40)	not null	
SEAT	Number	char(3)	not null	
	Aircraft registration number	char(20)	not null	**
	Smoking indicator	char(1)	not null	
	Position	char(6)	not null	
COUPON	Airline code	char(4)	not null	**
	Flight number	integer(4)	not null	**
	Date of departure	date	not null	**
	Date of issue	date	not null	**
	Passenger title	char(9)	not null	**
	Passenger surname	char(30)	not null	**
	Passenger initial	char(1)	not null	**
	Class	char(1)	not null	
	Status	char(2)	not null	
	Confirmed indicator	char(1)	not null	
	Comment	char(40)	null	
	Seat number	char(3)	null	**

Notice that the columns marked with ** are used to implement the relationships shown on the diagram by joining tables together. For example, the aircraft registration number is replicated on to the SEAT table to implement the relationship between the entities SEAT and AIRCRAFT. This column is known as a foreign key.

Not null is used to signify either a mandatory relationship (the solid line) or a mandatory attribute, as appropriate. **Null** is used to signify either an optional relationship (the dotted line) or an optional attribute – null means 'may have no value'.

Network Database

With a network database, each entity would typically be shown as a record type. Each relationship would normally become a set with some combination of Next, Prior and Owner pointers (NPO). Records requiring keyed access would be placed using a hashing algorithm (CALC). Records to be grouped together on the disk for performance reasons would be placed VIA some other record.

'MA' on the set is used to specify a Mandatory Automatic connection of say a SEAT record to an AIRCRAFT owner – used for mandatory relationships. 'OM' on the set is used to specify an Optional Manual connection for an optional relationship.

Figure 2-11
Network Design

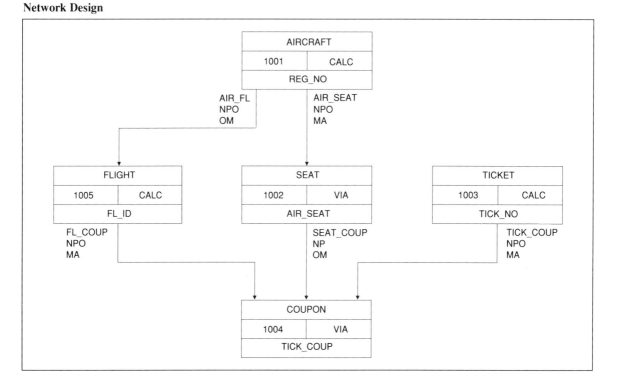

Hierarchic Database

With a hierarchic database, each entity would typically be shown as a record type, with some hierarchic subset of the entity model. Records would be arranged in a parent/child arrangement to satisfy what would normally be one to many relationships. Relationships are then implemented by some combination of logical (keyed) pointers or physical pointers. Where there is a network of information, such as where COUPON apparently appears at the bottom of three hierarchies, the concept of a virtual logical child ⌐ ↑ ⌐ is introduced, where pointers are used to cross to the real record required, which will be found in another hierarchy.

**Figure 2-12
Hierarchic Design**

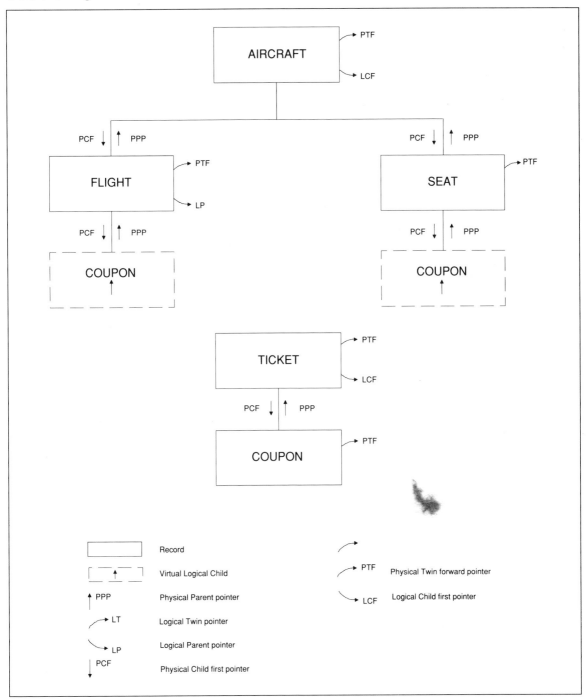

COBOL File

If the COBOL programming language was being used, the record layout for AIRCRAFT might have a repeating group for SEAT as shown below.

Figure 2-13
Layout of COBOL Record

```
    Record name    AIRCRAFT

    Fields:

02  AIR_NAME             PICTURE    X(40)
02  AIR_REG_NO           PICTURE    X(20)
02  AIR_TYPE             PICTURE    X(6)
02  AIR_DESC             PICTURE    X(40)
02  AIR_NUMBER_SEATS     PICTURE    9(3)
02  SEATS                OCCURS 0 TO 300 DEPENDING
                         ON AIR_NUMBER_SEATS
    04   SEAT_NO         PICTURE    X(3)
    04   SEAT_SMOKE_IND  PICTURE    X(1)


Note: the relationship SEAT on AIRCRAFT is now implemented
      by a repeating group on the aircraft record type, with
      AIR_NUMBER_SEATS used to limit occurrences.
```

Manual File

To complete the illustrations of databases, let us not forget that a large majority of data held in the world is stored in manual filing systems. The diagram opposite shows a possible implementation of a passenger (customer) file that might be held in a travel agency.

Figure 2-14
The Filing Cabinet!

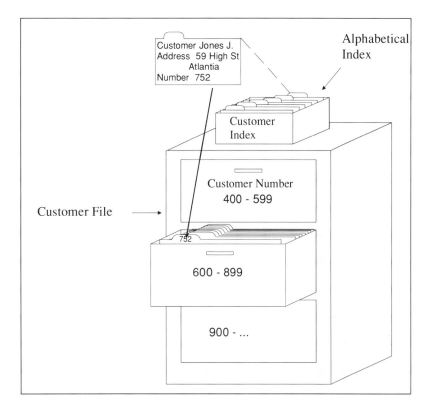

So What Have We Found?

Entity Relationship models can be used to represent the information needs of this example rigorously, where:

- A box represents an entity – a thing of significance about which information needs to be known or held. Entities have names and are described by attributes.

- Lines may be used to represent important business relationships between these things. Each relationship is given a name, degree (one or many) and optionality (optional/ mandatory) for each of its ends.

There has been a minimum definition, which has then been used in design to give the actual data structures needed.

Entity relationship models are constructed in a manner that is independent of any implementation technique. The paper and database examples illustrated how the requirement might be implemented.

And perhaps of most importance, the diagram acts as a definitive communication medium between the analyst and user, and between the analyst and designer.

Chapter

3

BASIC CONVENTIONS AND DEFINITIONS

This chapter covers the basic rules, conventions and definitions for entities, relationships, attributes and layout. Further details for reference are contained in Appendices B and C, and more advanced rules are covered in a later chapter and in Appendix A, which covers data normalization.

Entity

Entity Definition

An entity is a thing or object of significance, whether real or imagined, about which information needs to be known or held.

Figure 3-1
An Entity

ENTITY NAME

Entity Representation

An entity is represented diagrammatically by a softbox (i.e. a rectangle with rounded corners) with a name. The name is in the singular and shown in all capitals.

The softbox may be of any size or shape, sufficient to hold an unambiguous name (no abbreviations please) and to make the drawing of an Entity Relationship Diagram more convenient. It is often, for example, sensible to stretch a softbox to enable more relationship lines to connect to it without lines crossing unnecessarily or the diagram looking like a spider's web.

Entity Names

The name for an entity must be one that represents a type or class of thing – not an instance. In our case study, 'Heathrow' or 'John F. Kennedy' could not be names for entities – the entity is AIRPORT and those are two instances of this entity.

Synonyms may occur where there are different words to name an entity which have identical meanings within this business context. One name is chosen as the primary name; any synonyms may then be shown in capitals preceded by an oblique (/). Examples may then be shown in upper and lower case. Examples are essential to aid early understanding of this concept and to differentiate between similar concepts.

Figure 3-2
Example Entity

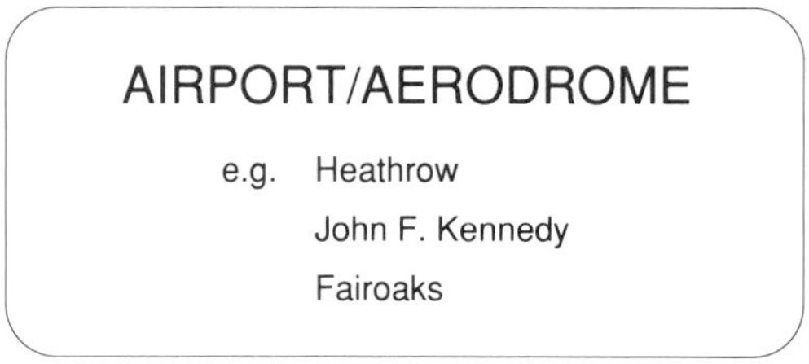

```
┌─────────────────────────────────────────┐
│                                           │
│        AIRPORT/AERODROME                  │
│                                           │
│      e.g.   Heathrow                      │
│             John F. Kennedy               │
│             Fairoaks                      │
│                                           │
└─────────────────────────────────────────┘
```

Fairoaks, by the way, is a small aerodrome in the south of England,
which nevertheless has a control tower, customs, immigration, etc.

Entity Rules

Any thing or object may only be represented by one entity. That is, entities are mutually exclusive in all cases.

Each entity must be uniquely identifiable.

That is, each instance (occurrence) of an entity must be separate and distinctly identifiable from all other instances of that type of entity.

(See Unique Identifier later in this chapter.)

Further advanced conventions and rules for entities are covered in Chapter 7. (See Appendix C for full details.)

Business Relationship

Relationship Definition

A business relationship, or relationship for short, is a named, significant association between two entities.

A relationship is binary, in the sense that it is always an association between exactly two named entities, or between an entity and itself.

Each relationship has two ends, for each of which there is a:

- name
- degree/cardinality (how many)
- optionality (optional or mandatory).

These properties are used to describe the association from one end; both ends must be defined.

Relationship Representation

A relationship is represented by a line that joins two entity softboxes together, or recursively joins one entity softbox to itself. The most common relationship is one that has a degree of **many to one**, is mandatory at the 'many' end and optional at the 'one' end as shown.

Figure 3-3
A Relationship

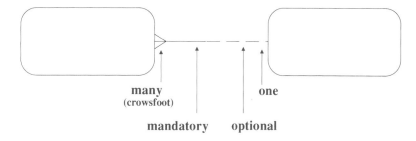

For a degree of **many**, the relationship line joins a softbox at three points, known as a 'crowsfoot'. For a degree of **one**, the line joins at only one point.

Where a relationship end is mandatory, a solid line is drawn for that half of the relationship. Where the relationship end is optional, a broken or dashed line is drawn.

It is often useful to think of a one to many relationship as being a parent to child relationship, with the existence of the child being in some way dependent on its parents.

Recursive Relationship

A recursive relationship with identical properties is shown below.

Figure 3-4
A Recursive Relationship

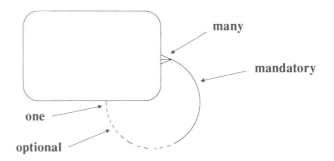

This particular recursive relationship shows an infinite hierarchy.

Naming Relationships

The name for each end of a relationship is placed near the appropriate end in lower case as shown below.

Figure 3-5
Naming a Relationship

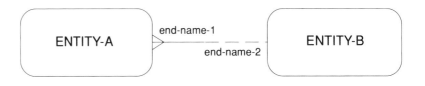

When the relationship end is mandatory the phrase 'must be' is used to precede the relationship end name; for optional relationship end names the phrase 'may be' is used.

Thus to read the diagram above from left to right one reads:

> *Each ENTITY-A must be end-name-1 one and only one ENTITY-B*

and from right to left:

> *Each ENTITY-B may be end-name-2 one or more ENTITY-A(s).*

This may seem fairly incomprehensible until you read an actual example.

Figure 3-6
An Example Relationship

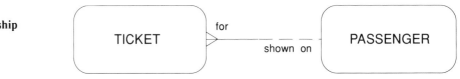

> *Each TICKET must be for one and only one PASSENGER and:*
> *Each PASSENGER may be shown on one or more TICKETs.*

The plural of the entity name is used when the degree is many. A degree of many is read as **one or more**, and a degree of one is read as **one and only one**.

When drawing Entity Relationship Diagrams, a higher degree of accuracy has been found if the crowsfeet (the many ends) can be placed to the left or the upper end of the relationship line. In addition, a naming technique that has the implied verb 'to be' has been shown to give more definitive and useful names.

Naming Discipline

Naming relationships, at both ends, helps eliminate unnecessary (redundant) relationships very early on, identifies weak understanding and frequently exposes the fact that further relationships and entities are needed.

A relationship definition is one that represents a **type** of association between two entities, to which all **instances** (occurrences) of relationships must conform. All the concepts in entity relationship modelling relate to types, not instances of those types.

Formal Syntax

To read any relationship simply but definitively the following syntax is used.

Each (and every) ENTITY-A $\left(\begin{array}{c} \textit{must be} \\ \\ \textit{may be} \end{array} \right)$ *end-name-1*

$\left(\begin{array}{c} \textit{ONE AND ONLY ONE ENTITY-B (ever)} \\ \\ \textit{ONE OR MORE ENTITY-B plural} \end{array} \right)$ *(is that true?)*

and conversely:

Each (and every) ENTITY-B $\left(\begin{array}{c} \textit{must be} \\ \\ \textit{may be} \end{array} \right)$ *end-name-2*

$\left(\begin{array}{c} \textit{ONE AND ONLY ONE ENTITY-A (ever)} \\ \\ \textit{ONE OR MORE ENTITY-A plural} \end{array} \right)$ *(is that true?)*

Notice that the words '*and every*' and '*ever*' can be inserted in the sentence to add even more rigour to it. The phrase '*and every*' implies that no instance of the entity can depart from the constraint applied by this relationship definition. The phrase '*ever*' implies that we are normally interested in relationships as they exist today, in the future and in the past.

The phrase '*is that true*' can be added to check the statement.

It we read the TICKET/PASSENGER relationship again this will become clear.

> *Each and every TICKET must be for one and only one PASSENGER ever, is that true?*

This is a good question, as the sentence implies that the company can never have tickets for families, groups or tickets when we do not know the identity of the passenger.

This ease of reading relationships in English and the degree of rigour is very important as it enables an analyst to tease out exceptions, time-related requirements and special cases at an early stage with the users. Having done so, the model can reflect those issues and subsequent system designs can then be chosen to provide the optimum mechanism to handle them (which includes manually). It has been found on many occasions that by far the majority of problems in maintenance occur because the designers did not know about these exceptions and the cost of re-working is then very high.

Inverted Syntax

The above syntax is very good for most purposes, but to really check out the details the following syntax may be useful.

Figure 3-7

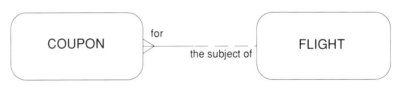

In normal syntax this is read as:

> *Each COUPON must be for one and only one FLIGHT ever.*

While in inverted syntax, it is read as:

> *That means you can never have a COUPON that is not for a uniquely identifiable FLIGHT, is that true?*

Here we have replaced 'each' by a much more questioning phrase, and the already delimiting phrase 'one and only one ... ever' by the phrase 'uniquely identifiable'.

Once more this is a good question, as the current model does not allow you to have a COUPON that does not uniquely identify a flight on a particular day. But in the real world open tickets do exist when the coupon does not show a specific departure date, and the relationship definition would need to be switched to optional to cater for this.

Valid Relationships

Not all relationships that may be drawn are valid or occur very often. The following are common relationship constructs.

Figure 3-8
**Common Valid
Relationships**

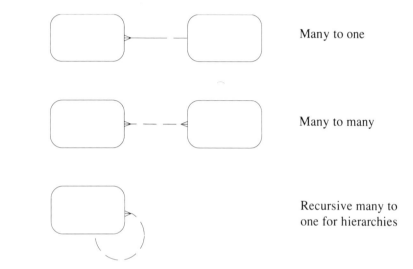

Many to one

Many to many

Recursive many to
one for hierarchies

The following are invalid, as they represent impossible conditions.

Figure 3-9
Invalid Relationships

Mandatory many to
many

Infinite hierarchy

Further conventions and rules for relationships are covered in Chapter 7, 'Advanced Conventions and Definitions'. Also see Appendix B for a comprehensive list of valid and invalid relationship constructs.

Attribute

Attribute Definition

An attribute is any detail that serves to qualify, identify, classify, quantify or express the state of an entity

or

Any description of a thing of significance.

An attribute could be text, numbers, a picture, a feel, a smell, and so on, as required. For data processing purposes we tend to concentrate on text and numbers, but other attribute types could be critical to the success of running your business; for example, the professionalism of members of the Information Systems Department.

Attribute Representation

To represent an attribute, write its name in the singular in lower case, optionally with an example of its value.

Figure 3-10
Adding the Attributes

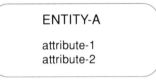

On an Entity Relationship Diagram it is not necessary to show attributes, but adding one or two to each entity during the formative period is highly beneficial. In particular, this is useful when distinguishing between entities for 'type' and 'instance'.

In the following example, candidate attributes are essential to help us distinguish between two entities.

Figure 3-11

In our case study the airline may have acquired only four or five different aircraft types, but may have a hundred or more actual aircraft. The attribute registration number would have a value unique to each instance of the entity AIRCRAFT.

Attribute Rules

The following simple rules help us create an accurate, complete and flexible model. See also Appendix A, 'Data Normalization'.

An Attribute Describes One Entity

The attribute must describe the entity against which it is shown!

This may seem obvious, but it is the most common error found with attributes. For example, is 'seat number' an attribute of a coupon, ticket, boarding pass, aircraft or seat on an aircraft? It is obviously an attribute of SEAT, but in real life we often see the number replicated many times; for example, on a boarding pass, which is shown as an entity in its own right in Figure 3-12.

Why? In the real world a seat number is a very convenient way of representing a relationship. When you find these situations, draw in the relationship line instead (if necessary creating the entity to which it refers) as illustrated below.

Figure 3-12
Assigning an Attribute to the Correct Entity

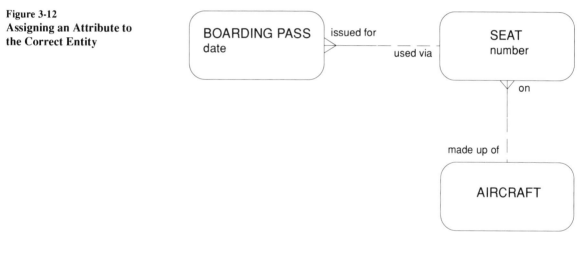

As a guide, most entities will only be described by between two and eight attributes. If you have more than this, there are probably many relationships and/or entities missing.

Reading Attribute Names

Do not use the entity name as part of the attribute name. It would be redundant, as the attribute only describes the one entity. In the above example, 'seat number' actually helped us identify a missing entity called SEAT, which could then be described by the attribute 'number' and perhaps other attributes such as 'type'.

To read attributes that are named in this manner, you can use one of two forms:

>entity name attribute name
>
>or   attribute name of entity name,

for example, seat number or number of seat.

In the classic example of employees and their departments, 'department number' is not an attribute of the entity EMPLOYEE. It is an attribute of DEPARTMENT, and should then be defined as number of department.

Remove Repeated
Attributes
(First Normal Form)

An entity may only have one value for an attribute at any time. If multiple values are essential, you must create a new entity to hold them with a many to one relationship to the original entity. Using the seat example again, an early model might have been:

Figure 3-13
A Repeated Attribute
Indicates a Missing Entity

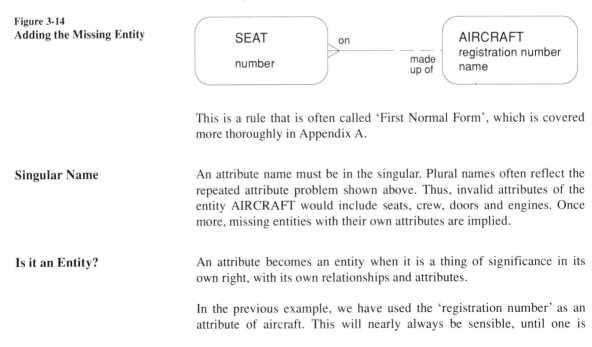

Following the above rule we get:

Figure 3-14
Adding the Missing Entity

This is a rule that is often called 'First Normal Form', which is covered more thoroughly in Appendix A.

Singular Name

An attribute name must be in the singular. Plural names often reflect the repeated attribute problem shown above. Thus, invalid attributes of the entity AIRCRAFT would include seats, crew, doors and engines. Once more, missing entities with their own attributes are implied.

Is it an Entity?

An attribute becomes an entity when it is a thing of significance in its own right, with its own relationships and attributes.

In the previous example, we have used the 'registration number' as an attribute of aircraft. This will nearly always be sensible, until one is considering the registration sub-system of an airline, in which case we may also need the 'date of registration', 'where it was registered', 'what was it registered for?', 're-registered aircraft?', and so on. Our diagram would then start to evolve into something like the following:

**Figure 3-15
An Attribute may
Become an Entity**

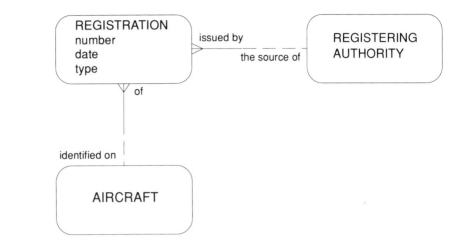

Beware! It is easy to get carried away into irrelevant detail. In this case we are **not** interested in this sub-system and will revert to the previous model, perhaps improving our understanding by adding the adjective 'current' to the registration number.

Figure 3-16

```
┌─────────────────────────────────────┐
│                                      │
│            AIRCRAFT                  │
│                                      │
│      current registration number     │
│                                      │
└─────────────────────────────────────┘
```

Unique Identifier

Each entity must be uniquely identifiable by a combination of attribute(s) and/or relationships (see later in this chapter). Thus one should always seek out any candidate attributes that help to identify an entity.

On your car (or these aeroplanes we have been considering) the use of chassis numbers, engine numbers, and so on, is obviously potentially of value.

Attribute Value Must be Dependent on the Whole Unique Identifier
(Second Normal Form)

Remove those attributes for which the values are dependent on only part of the unique identifier. This is known as 'Second Normal Form', and is covered in Appendix A. Such attributes normally imply a missing but related entity.

Attributes Must be Dependent on the Unique Identifier
(Third Normal Form)

Remove those attributes that are not dependent on the unique identifier of the entity. This is known as Third Normal Form. For example, one might have a boarding pass on which the passenger's name is recorded.

"Is the passenger's name dependent in any way on the unique identifier of the boarding pass?"

Obviously not. (Well, I don't change **my** name when I get issued with a boarding pass!) If the attribute is **not** dependent on the unique identifier, there is probably a missing entity and/or relationship.

Optional Attributes

An attribute may have a value for only some of the time, or the value may not be available. In which case, this may be shown by a small 'o' in front of the attribute name to indicate that it is optional.

Mandatory Attributes

The value of an attribute which must always be known is shown by a small '*' in front of the name. But be careful – applied rigorously this means that on no occasion would you know of the existence of an entity occurrence without knowing the value of each of its mandatory attributes. Now that's what I call really rigorous! In practical use, this degree of rigour is normally relaxed slightly.

**Figure 3-17
Showing the Optionality of Attributes**

FLIGHT

* date of departure
° time of departure

Unique Identifier

Definition

Each entity must be uniquely identifiable so that each instance of the entity is separate and distinctly identifiable from all other instances of that type of entity. The unique identifier may be an attribute, a combination of attributes, a combination of relationships or a combination of attribute(s) and relationship(s).

An entity may have more than one alternative means of unique identification. The primary method may be shown on the Entity Relationship Diagram by preceding an attribute that contributes to the identifier with a '#' mark and placing a bar across contributing relationship line(s).

Figure 3-18
Showing Unique Identifiers

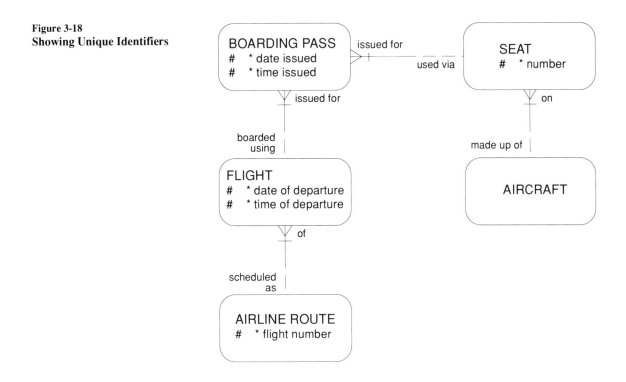

Thus, to uniquely identify a boarding pass, one needs:

- the relationship to the seat, and thus its seat number
- the relationship to the flight, and thus its date/time of departure
- the date/time issued in the rare case of boarding passes being re-issued; for example, to re-seat a family closer together after someone did not turn up for the flight
- as the unique identifier of the flight also includes the relationship to the airline route, we also need the flight number.

Type and Instance

It is important to understand that the definitions we have just looked at for entity, relationship, attribute and unique identifier are all definitions that represent a type or class of concept – not an instance. Let us have a look at part of the case study to see what we mean.

Figure 3-19

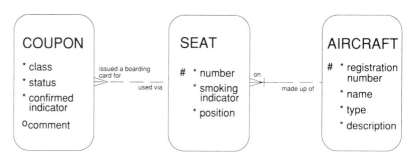

The above diagram of types or classes of objects can be visualized in three dimensions, like stacks of cards in a filing system, to show the actual instances.

Figure 3-20
Snapshot of Instances

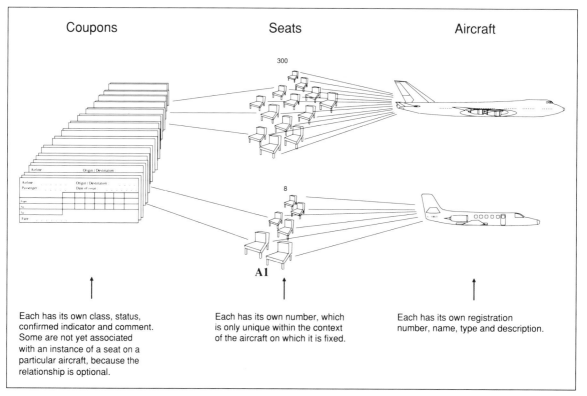

Each has its own class, status, confirmed indicator and comment. Some are not yet associated with an instance of a seat on a particular aircraft, because the relationship is optional.

Each has its own number, which is only unique within the context of the aircraft on which it is fixed.

Each has its own registration number, name, type and description.

All the seats are associated with an aircraft, but only some have coupons so far. This picture, therefore, only represents a snapshot of the real world, in which empty seats on an aircraft are valid.

When we look at **all** the coupons, past, current and those that have already been pre-allocated for future flights, we see the following situation.

Figure 3-21
Future, Current and
History of Instances

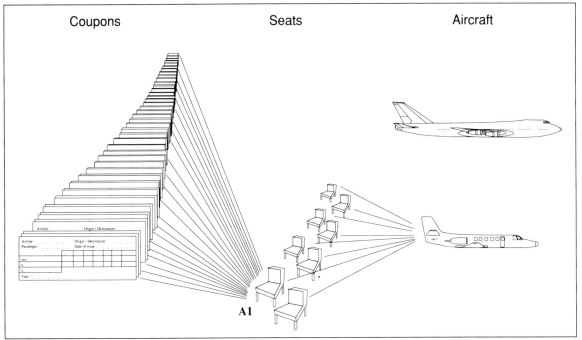

The seat to aircraft picture has not changed, but we now have hundreds of thousands more coupons from which we have selected all those ever allocated (past, current or pre-allocated) to seat A1 on the aircraft with the registration number G-ORCE.

Your definitions must equally accurately apply to each and every instance of the object – not just the normal case. In our case study the fleet of aircraft may include a couple of very old ones, for which it is vital to know when the availability of spare parts was last checked. In such an exceptional case, if it is very important, the definitions must cater for the information required **as an option** that will not apply in the normal case.

All the other concepts and definitions in entity relationship modelling also apply to the type or class of object.

Layout Rules

The simple layout rules that follow are designed to make the diagrams easy to read, applicable to the people who need to work with them and to maximize the quality and accuracy.

Subset Diagrams

When discussing a particular functional area with a user or a design issue with your designers, it is a good idea to create a subset diagram and lay it out again to act most effectively as a communication vehicle for that purpose. In the process you will often find omissions and errors, which can then be quickly corrected – the different perspective is a powerful analytical tool.

Neat and Tidy

Arrange your diagram so the entity boxes line up, and relationship lines are mainly straight and horizontal or vertical. Minimize crossing lines. When relationship lines must cross, try to use an angle between them in the range of thirty to sixty degrees, which makes it easier for the eye to follow along the lines.

Beware of constructing a diagram with large numbers of closely parallel lines: these make it difficult to follow. Use plenty of white space to avoid the feeling of congestion and the occasional diagonal line to help the aesthetics of the diagram.

Labelling

Add a title and date, and identify the author(s) of each diagram.

Pattern Recognition

Most people have an in-built ability to recognize shapes and patterns in an instant and thus can easily remember the subject matter. Modellers can take advantage of this, making each diagram distinctly different in shape (size does not seem to affect the issue). Later, a previously agreed model can be discussed again with maximum productivity.

The corollary of this is that if you produce several diagrams with the same shape or pattern this ability to quickly recall the detail is lost.

Text

Ensure that all the text is unambiguous. Avoid abbreviations and jargon. Use the reading conventions described earlier and read all around a diagram to ensure that it is complete and accurate. A good Entity Relationship Diagram should be semantically complete. Add adjectives and examples when reading it, if necessary, to improve understanding and accuracy.

Most of the text should be horizontally aligned to make it easier to read. You may use more than one line for a name to ease layout problems. If necessary write the relationship names along the lines, but normally you should put the names at the ends of the line and on opposite sides of the line.

Figure 3-22

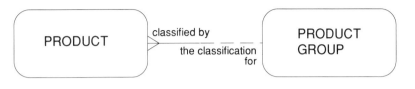

Centre, left align or right align the text consistently for a high quality deliverable.

Relationship Degree

Arrange for the many end (crowsfoot) of relationships to be on the left or at the top of the relationship line. This technique has been found to increase the accuracy of the model by forcing consideration of the relationships from the more frequently occurring entities towards the less frequent.

(Most people read diagrams from left to right and from top to bottom, so this follows the natural path. This is helped by the fact that those things there are fewest of, which will appear at the bottom right-hand of the diagram, are highly significant entities that are used to define other things; for example, company, product, airport. Thus, reading towards them helps us define the other entities in part by their relationship to these reference entities.)

Entity Size and Shape

There is no special significance given to the size or shape of an entity. Thus boxes may be stretched, enlarged or shrunk to help the layout of the diagram.

Figure 3-23
A Typical Layout

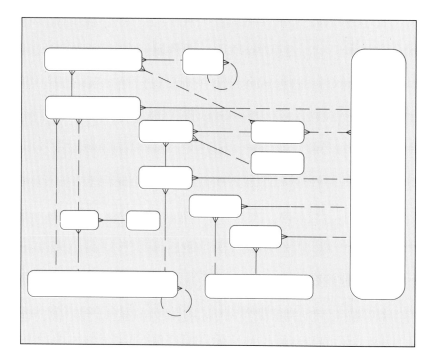

Notice that two diagonal lines have been used, purely to break the otherwise slightly precise feeling, and it still obeys the guideline of 'many above and to the left'.

Quality

When using these conventions, similar entities tend to appear in adjacent positions on the diagram. This has proved very useful in practice, as they are often the same thing but under different names – examine their attributes, relationships and the business functions that use them.

Further Conventions

This chapter has covered the basic conventions and definitions required for entity relationship modelling. The next chapter covers a further example and introduces additional concepts. Detailed definitions, further rules and quality checks are then covered for these more sophisticated conventions, which will enable you to model more complex situations.

Chapter

4

A SECOND EXAMPLE

We have worked through a simple example on airlines and seen the conventions and definitions that apply. Let us now have a look at a different example and introduce a new concept.

Credit cards (or charge cards) seem to appear in every situation one can imagine, sourced from banks, shops and even the airlines of our previous example. In this second example we must consider them from the viewpoint of the credit card company.

The Example

The credit card company sets up accounts against either named individuals or a client company, which may be issuing cards for its employees. The credit card company issues three different types of card, with different limits, payment terms and other conditions.

Under either personal or corporate accounts there may well be many cards authorized. It is important to know who has each. Physically this is achieved by embossing the name of the card holder on the card, along with the account number and expiry date. (Why not have a look at a card that you may have to help you visualize the situation?)

You may have an account, with a card for yourself and one for your spouse. Your company may also have an account with a card for you – don't get them confused when paying for your holiday!

Your spouse could even own a third account with cards for both of you and your children – these cards can be given very low limits. A wise precaution perhaps?

The credit card company needs to know who owns accounts, who has cards and how many cards of different types are held in personal or corporate accounts.

Let us analyze the words and find the entities, attributes and relationships to model this example.

The First Paragraph of the Example

> *The credit card company sets up accounts against either named individuals or a client company, which may be issuing cards for its employees. The credit card company issues three different types of card, with different limits, payment terms and other conditions.*

Looking at this first paragraph we find some useful nouns, which we convert to the singular:

- company
- account
- individual
- card (or perhaps credit card is better)
- employee.

Perhaps these are entities, as they are all significant things.

We have also got some other nouns and expressions:

- type of card
- limit
- payment term
- condition.

Perhaps some of these are attributes, as they would be useful words to describe other things. Try to work out which entity they might refer to.

Is type of card an attribute of card or an entity in its own right? If it is an entity it must be a thing of significance about which information needs to be known or held. In this case it is, because limit and payment term are some of its attributes. We will call it CARD TYPE. An instance of a CARD TYPE could be one where the limit is two hundred dollars and the payment term requires payment in full at the end of the month – ideal for my children, each of whom might have a card of this type.

Are there any possible relationships? These will be found between pairs of entities as link phrases:

COMPANY sets up ACCOUNTs
ACCOUNTs against INDIVIDUAL or against COMPANY
COMPANY for its EMPLOYEEs.

These may not all be relationships and we have COMPANY appearing twice – once as the credit card company and once as the company for which we work. Let us assume that the credit card company is simply the context for this example and ignore it for now.

Notice that we have an **either/or** situation with ACCOUNTs. We need a new convention called the exclusive relationship to handle this, as illustrated in the diagram below by the arc across two relationship ends on the diagram.

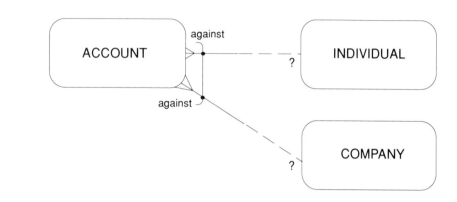

We read this as:

> *Each ACCOUNT must be against either one and only one INDIVIDUAL or against one and only one COMPANY (ever).*

This little sub-model is incomplete, but a useful guide. It is drawn with a relationship of many to one from ACCOUNT because it was ACCOUNTs (plural) to COMPANY (singular). The relationship name end on the other end has not yet been added and you may want to improve the words later.

The Second Paragraph

> *Under either personal or corporate accounts there may well be many cards authorized. It is important to know who has each. Physically this is achieved by embossing the name of the card holder on the card, along with the account number and expiry date. (Why not have a look at a card that you may have to help you visualize the situation.)*

Once again look for nouns:

- personal account
- corporate account
- card holder.

Possible attributes are:

- name of card holder
- account number
- expiry date.

Notice how they conform to the way in which attributes should be read:

entity name attribute name
or
attribute name of entity name.

Possible relationships in this paragraph are:

Under PERSONAL ACCOUNT ... CARDs

Under CORPORATE ACCOUNT ... CARDs

This is interesting, as it was not at all obvious from the words. If we put CARDs at the front it then reads:

CARDs under PERSONAL ACCOUNT

which now looks like a many to one relationship from CARD to ACCOUNT.

The Remaining Paragraphs   Possible entities are:

- account
- card
- spouse
- company
- child
- credit company
- card of type (card type).

Possible attributes are:

- very low limit.

Possible relationships are:

- ACCOUNT with CARD
- COMPANY have ACCOUNT
- CARD for YOU
- SPOUSE own ACCOUNT
- CARDs for CHILDREN
- CARDs of different TYPEs.

Synthesis

We now have a lot of useful information. Let us apply some logic to help us.

How many people can be named on a card? Only one on all the cards I have seen.

Could someone have more than one account? There seems no reason why they should not have.

Now look at the possible entity names. Several of them are really the same sort of thing:

- individual
- employee
- card holder
- spouse
- child.

Are they mutually exclusive in all situations, or could the same thing be an employee, card holder, spouse and child? If so, we need a new generic word – in this case PERSON. The other words are examples or roles of person. Some of these words may appear again as relationship names.

Now spend ten minutes or so and try to construct an Entity Relationship Diagram from the above information.

Once you have finished the model, check it with your colleagues using the guidelines given and then guess additional attributes. To help you get started, have a look at a credit card of your own – it will have attributes such as:

- valid from date
- expiry date
- date issued
- signature.

Everything else on the card should be a relationship or replicated data that applies to that type of card.

How would you uniquely identify a card?

Compare your rough model with the solution on the next page.

Credit Card Solution

Figure 4-2
Entity Relationship Model
for the Credit Card Example

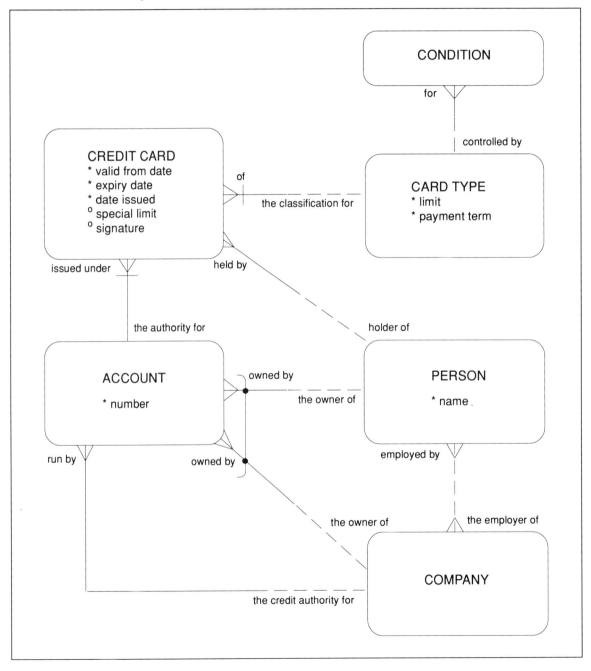

Read through the diagram to check that it caters for the following possible situations.

From PERSON go to ACCOUNT and then to say two instances of cards, one held by you and one held by your spouse.

Similarly, the solution should cater for your spouse's account with cards for you, your spouse and each child.

Starting at COMPANY we can find the ACCOUNTs it owns, with the CREDIT CARDs issued under it, and thus we can find anyone who is a corporate card holder. Notice that 'holder of' as a relationship name came from the 'card holder' role.

CARD TYPE is a separate entity with a parent to child relationship to another entity called CONDITION. There would be many terms and conditions for a CARD TYPE, so CONDITION cannot be an attribute of CARD TYPE as it would break the rule that an attribute can only have one value at any one time.

From CARD TYPE we can find all CREDIT CARDs of that type and then locate the related ACCOUNTs, which are the authority for them, and thus get to either individual owners or corporate owners. We can therefore determine how many cards of different types are held in personal or corporate accounts.

Who owns the ACCOUNTs is found simply by going along the 'owned by' relationships.

For completeness, the credit card company itself is shown as a possible occurrence of the entity COMPANY by the relationship from ACCOUNT run by/credit authority for COMPANY. This structure even allows the model to be used for more than one credit card company, and for the credit card company to have an account for its own staff.

A many to many relationship between PERSON and COMPANY allows us to know who works where, in case we want to check for CREDIT CARDs under corporate ACCOUNTs being issued to people who are not employees (e.g. the company president's spouse).

Notice that each ACCOUNT **must be** authority for at least one CREDIT CARD. This results from the application of a business rule that says it makes no sense to set up an account without at least one card. (This may or may not be true.)

The signature attribute on CREDIT CARD is optional because there is a gap in time after issue before the card holder has a chance to sign it.

And finally, although we have a limit by CARD TYPE, we have also added a special limit as an attribute of CREDIT CARD to allow an override for a particular PERSON.

Conclusion

Even with just a few entities and a little information one may construct very sophisticated and rigorous models. Exclusive relationships, shown by an arc, can be very useful.

Finally, there were some useful business functions here, each of which acts on entities. Modelling of business functions is covered in other publications, but a few are listed below.

Set up account for individual person or company.

Issue card to person under an account.

Set limits, payment terms and create conditions for card types.

Identify credit card by card holder, account and expiry date.

Analyze credit cards by type.

Identify any card for which the expiry date is next month and reissue card to person under the account.

Chapter

5

IDENTIFYING ENTITIES, ATTRIBUTES AND RELATIONSHIPS

In general, the rigorous use of the definitions is all that anyone needs to identify entities, attributes and relationships, but in practice there are some mechanistic ways to help you during your learning curve. Some of the techniques were illustrated in the previous chapter, and you may find it useful to read it again after this one.

The words entity, attribute and relationship are defined in all good dictionaries and have been used in the way we use them for hundreds of years. The Glossary includes a dictionary definition for your interest.

Identifying Entities

Entities are things people talk about, write about, record information about and do work on – by definition.

An entity is a thing or object of significance, whether real or imagined, about which information needs to be known or held.

That definition is useful – it makes our job a lot easier as entities are to be found virtually anywhere as the nouns in sentences.

So why is it sometimes difficult to identify them?

**Examples, Synonyms,
Homonyms and Roles**

The answer to this is simple. People often talk in terms of examples, analogies and by illustrations. Instead of talking about **aircraft** they talk about jumbo jets, 747s and Concorde.

To further confuse us, people frequently use synonyms. A synonym is another word with the same meaning, so for aircraft a common synonym might be aeroplane.

Homonyms are where the same word can have more than one meaning, depending on the context, and often within the same sentence! The word program (or programme, depending on your spelling preference) nowadays has a multitude of alternative meanings, such as:

- a set of instructions for a computer
- a series of events
- a course of study
- a plan of intention
- a description of the proceedings at a musical concert
- what you could be watching on your television if you weren't reading this.

People often talk in terms of the roles of the things, particularly of people and organizations. These roles are sometimes job titles, sometimes informal responsibilities and sometimes names that we attach to people simply because of the way in which we come into contact with them. Here are some examples of roles of person:

manager, clerk, secretary, safety officer, mother, leader, chairman of a group, trainer, airline pilot, politician, guru, receptionist, child, engine driver, fall-guy, counsellor, scientist, janitor, clown, air traffic controller, ecologist.

Plurals and other grammatical terms add a further layer of confusion for us to cut through. And finally, even within the same language the spelling of words may vary between countries; for example, aeroplane/airplane; colour/color; sulphur/sulfur.

None of these alternative names invented by man changes what a thing is intrinsically.

*"What's in a name? that which we call a rose
By any other name would smell as sweet."*
William Shakespeare

Our job is to identify the essential underlying thing, select a generic word for it that everyone is happy with, and then define that entity. In the process we may well keep a whole set of synonyms and examples for the object to help with clarity.

For Example

The entity named LOCOMOTIVE has a synonym TRAIN, and examples of the entity are The Flying Scotsman, Puffing Billy, Stephenson's Rocket and, a somewhat more recent example, the Japanese monorail Bullet.

Analyzing an Interview

Let us have a look at a transcript of an interview conducted by an analyst and then see if you can determine how the entities were derived.

Q. *Tell me about the different ways people can book tickets.*

A. *Most of the time someone would ring up a travel agent and discuss the journey they want to make.*

Sometimes it's very clear. They simply want to catch the British Airways 747 to Paris on a particular date. More often, though, they would discuss the pros and cons of going by different airlines, at different times, possibly landing at a different airport – executives can even charter a plane and land at a local aerodrome or landing strip.

The agent, possibly one of ours, will try to work out a schedule that most closely matches the required part of the day they wish to arrive, check that there is room on the flights, book the passengers on, possibly allocate seats and then issue tickets.

A common example is like yesterday when this man came in and asked for an open ticket from here to San Francisco, any time after the tenth of June, so that he could get the best airfare possible and then organize his trip later.

.....

The other problem we frequently have is when another package tour operator asks for a block booking for say 20 seats, at a discount. It is often not until the last minute that we know their customers and can fill in their names on the tickets.

.....

If you analyze the conversation above and then define generic words in the singular for the things you find, the result may look something like this.

Generic Word	Source
Company	travel agent airline British Airways package tour operator
Aircraft	747 plane
City	Paris San Francisco
Airport	Paris aerodrome landing strip San Francisco
Schedule	schedule
Period	day/date June part of day
Person	executives agent passenger man customer
Booking	block booking
Ticket	tickets open ticket
Journey	trip
Flight	flight
Seat	seats

The nouns airfare, discount and name are almost certainly attributes of other entities.

Paper Sources

You could also analyze written documents in a similar manner. Of particular value are annual reports from companies, which often prove a fruitful source of really significant reference entities.

Paper forms may prove useful, although they tend to be a better source for attributes, as the sections that you fill in are nearly always preceded by the name of the attribute.

Common Sense

Finally, look around you when you are in the context of the part of the organization being analyzed. Most of the things you see will turn out to be instances of entities.

In our example, imagine you are in a travel agent's office – what would you see? Obviously – desks, chairs, a counter, telephones, doors, windows, and so on.

These may not be significant unless you are considering requirements from an asset, inventory or physical resource perspective.

On the other hand the following may well prove to be very important:

- brochures
- timetables
- maps
- booking forms
- credit term details
- the bureau de change
- and so on.

Whether they need to be modelled you must determine with your users or by extrapolation of existing systems or procedures that must be catered for.

Using your abilities of observation, common sense and logical powers of deduction will add real value to the quality of your models.

Remember, every entity must be uniquely identifiable and must have at least two attributes (none of which are relationships!) before you have completed your analysis. Therefore the following very direct question is useful:

"How do you uniquely identify a ....?"

Identifying Attributes

Attributes are the information we need to know about things.

Often these will appear as data in a computer or manual system – so obviously this is a good source. Use it for 'bottom-up' checking to ensure that you have not missed any attributes from other sources such as interviews.

Remember, an attribute is:

any detail that serves to qualify, identify, classify, quantify or express the state of an entity
or
any description of a thing.

Ask!

When you have identified an entity, by far the easiest thing to do is to ask a user:

"What information do you need to know or hold about ....?"

Unfortunately they will give you answers that contain other concepts as well, so you still have to analyze the answer in detail. Remember the definitions and be really rigorous.

Paper Forms

Potential attributes are easily found by examining paper forms. Take the headings and prompts from blank forms. Also analyze forms that have been filled in, and look for those extra pieces of information recorded on the back, in the notes sections or clipped on to the form in question. But be careful. The same attribute can often appear under different names on different forms.

Computer Files

Computer files, COBOL definitions, database schemas, screen layouts, and so on, provide a wealth of data that can be analyzed. Data normalization techniques may be used to help. (See Appendix A.) In practice, the same data will recur many times with acronyms, abbreviations and prefixes according to the whim of the original programmer, or as required to conform to the standards of the installation or to fit within the constraints of the software, such as 8-character names.

There is a danger that by analyzing paper forms and existing computer files you may restate obsolete systems as new requirements. To avoid this, always model the need first, based on interviews, and then check existing systems for omissions. Once this bottom-up check has been performed go back to the user with questions such as, *"Is this still really needed?"*

Examples and Identifiers

If you read through the interview extract again, you can now use many of the examples to indicate attributes that might apply, such as:

	Attribute of	Entity
British Airways	name	company
747	type	aircraft
Paris	name	city
	name	airport

Notice that **British Airways** is probably a potential unique identifier for a company that is an airline.

747 could be an attribute of aircraft, or it could indicate that we need a new entity called AIRCRAFT TYPE, where 747 would be a value of its attribute named 'code'.

AIRCRAFT TYPE   code – **e.g. 747**
                       description
                       maximum loaded weight.

Quoted Attributes

From the interview you will notice that many attributes are quoted directly, but tying them to their entities has to be achieved. Simply ask yourself, *"What does it describe?"*

What does 'airfare' describe?	The ticket or possibly it is the standard 'airfare' for a route.
What does 'date' describe?	Flight or booking.
What might 'discount' apply to?	Again the ticket, and possibly some form of standard agreement for bulk bookings – a missing entity perhaps?

Derived Data

On both computer files and paper systems there will be derived data of many sorts – in particular on reports or summary screens. With entity relationship modelling we rarely want to record derivable data, as long as we have identified all the attributes from which it was derived.

The primary exception would be when the business needs to keep summary information for a much longer period of time than the data from which it is derivable. In this case, define a new entity for the summary information and give it attributes and business functions to create it. Other exceptions are when business functions frequently reference derived data; for example, the number of seats on an aircraft.

Identifying Relationships

Relationships are mainly implied in conversation, on manual forms or explicitly supported by computer systems.

A relationship is a named significant association between two things.

Again, ask!

You can use the same simple technique of asking people questions such as:

"Could you tell me all the different ways a person could be associated with a ticket?"

The answer will probably be very long but useful in more ways than you intended, and you will probably get words like:

- – passenger on the ticket
- – booked by
- – changed by
- – inspected by
- – issued by.

Now these are all potentially useful and open up the area of investigation again.

Analyze Interviews

Go through the interview extract again, and this time look for link phrases between nouns – they can often suggest relationships.

Phrase	Becomes
British Airways 747 to Paris	FLIGHT to AIRPORT
Executives charter plane	AIRCRAFT chartered by PERSON
Agent ... work out schedule	SCHEDULE prepared by PERSON
Ticket from here to San Francisco	TICKET originating from AIRPORT and terminating at AIRPORT

Then you need to ask questions to check on the degree and optionality discussed previously.

Paper or Computer Forms

These are often laid out in a structure such as that shown opposite.

Figure 5-1
Blank Form

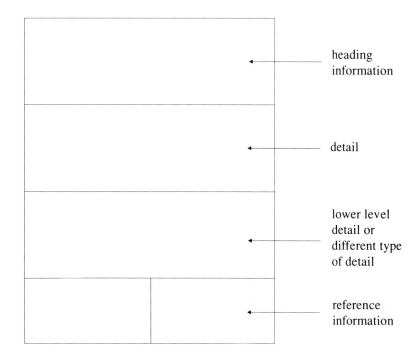

heading
information

detail

lower level
detail or
different type
of detail

reference
information

Each of the actual or implied lines across such a form may well help you
identify a relationship. You have to identify it first and then name it.

Figure 5-2
Possible Implied Entity
Relationship Model from the
Above Form

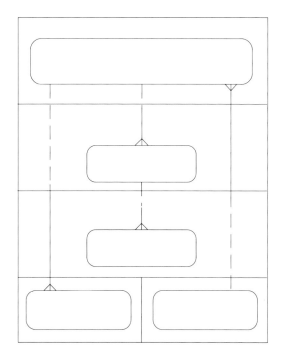

In some cases it is more complex, as each zone of the form may also reference another reference entity and so it may be as complex as follows.

Figure 5-3
Complex Implied
Relationship

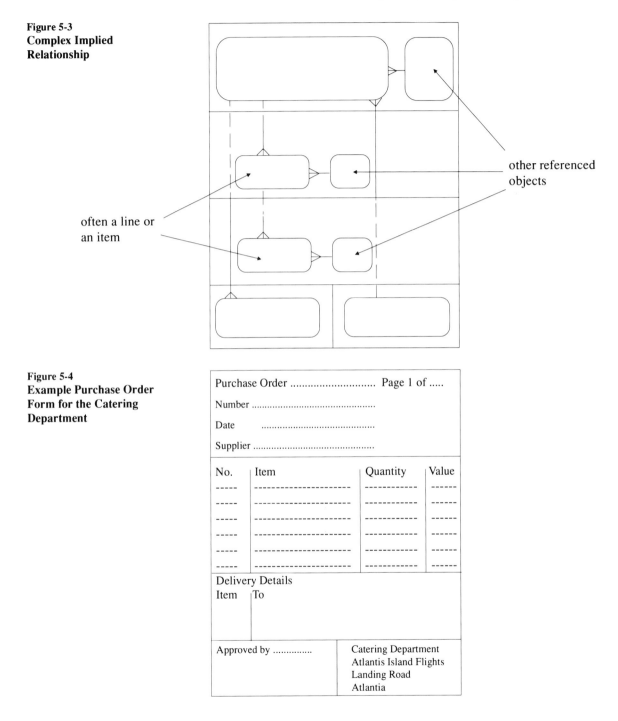

other referenced
objects

often a line or
an item

Figure 5-4
Example Purchase Order
Form for the Catering
Department

Purchase Order .... Page 1 of .....

Number ....

Date   ....

Supplier ....

No.	Item	Quantity	Value
-----	---------------------	------------	------
-----	---------------------	------------	------
-----	---------------------	------------	------
-----	---------------------	------------	------
-----	---------------------	------------	------
-----	---------------------	------------	------

Delivery Details
Item   To

Approved by ....   Catering Department
Atlantis Island Flights
Landing Road
Atlantia

On the example classic purchase order form opposite there are relationships from:

Purchase Order	to	Line (from the multiple lines that reference an item)
Line	to	Item (or Product)
Delivery	to	Item or Purchase Order
Purchase Order	approved by	Person
Purchase Order	to	Supplier
Purchase Order	to	Catering Department (an example of a purchasing department).

Only one relationship was named, but you can now derive a model such as the one drawn below to illustrate how it covers the information on the example form.

Figure 5-5
Implied Model for
Purchase Order Form

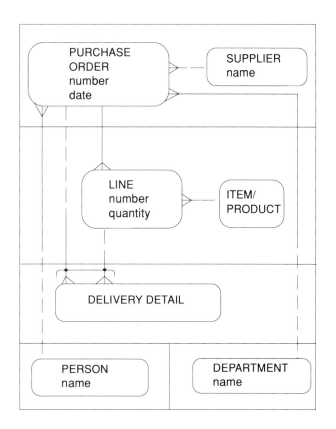

Why not try to add relationship names, check whether the degree and optionality shown for each relationship is sensible and try out this technique on other forms.

Grid Technique

Lay out all the entity names as the headings in a grid, as below, and then put names in the boxes where they are significantly related. Notice that there may be several associations between two entities.

	PERSON				
PERSON	hundreds possible	AIRCRAFT			
AIRCRAFT	flown by serviced by	alternative to	TICKET		
TICKET	booked by passenger for	?	replaced by	BOOKING	
BOOKING	made by made for	for	issued by	subordinate to	PURCHASE ORDER
PURCHASE ORDER	approved by	?	–	–	under?
etc.					

This can suggest a lot of useful questions about possible relationships, but it can also cause you to define relationships that are redundant, which you will subsequently have to remove. (See Chapter 7.)

Computer Files

Finally, analyzing the structure of computer files for systems that need to be replaced gives many insights. Work with a database designer who understands the current system and look for:

– pointers
– foreign keys
– repeating groups
– structured codes

all of which imply possible relationships.

Summary

To reach maximum potential, it is important for any analyst to understand the meaning of words, to have a rich vocabulary, to define everything important that is met and to listen carefully to what is actually said.

The art of translating what is said into a generic model of the underlying structure takes a little practice. With the guidance of this book and the use of constant feedback to users and your colleagues, you can scientifically turn these jumbles of words into definitive models of your users' information needs.

Chapter

6

A COMPLEX EXAMPLE

Let us return to Atlantis Island Flights and cater for some more common modelling situations.

Atlantis Island Flights
(the continuing story)

To maintain a flexible service to its clients, Atlantis Island Flights enables clients to acquire tickets with open coupons. This applies to those who regularly fly on a specific route and want to have prepaid tickets that they can use on any date. It also applies, in particular, to the return journey on a trip of indefinite duration.

Figure 6-1
An Open Ticket

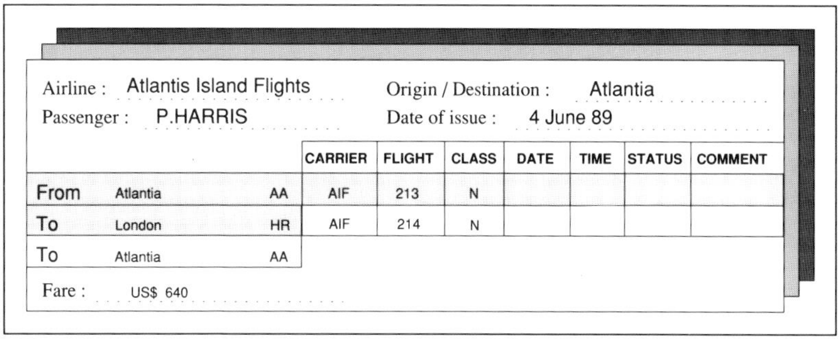

			CARRIER	FLIGHT	CLASS	DATE	TIME	STATUS	COMMENT
From	Atlantia	AA	AIF	213	N				
To	London	HR	AIF	214	N				
To	Atlantia	AA							

Airline : Atlantis Island Flights   Origin / Destination : Atlantia
Passenger : P.HARRIS   Date of issue : 4 June 89

Fare : US$ 640

Flights, by the way, fall into two categories – those regular scheduled flights and those which are non-scheduled.

Special tickets are allocated to the airline staff. These are simply shown as normal open tickets, with a colour stripe across the coupon. As a matter of company policy no more than ten staff, and within that 5 crew members, can travel on any flight as passengers. It is also important to know who they are and what their jobs are, for emergency use. Staff tickets have no associated fare, when travelling on behalf of the company. When travelling as private citizens the same rules apply and their tickets show the full price, along with the staff discount. (Other discounts may apply from time to time in other circumstances.)

Crew membership must be controlled rigorously to ensure the appropriate level of skill and numbers of different types of job. Normally this is controlled by having a predefined list of jobs that must be filled on every passenger-carrying flight, dependent only on the type of aircraft.

Figure 6-2
A Crew Roster

CREW ROSTER -	Flight	AIF 213	
	Date	**26th August 1989**	
	Aircraft	**BOEING 747**	
Crew Members	Name	Title	Comment
Flight Crew - Captain - Second Pilot - Navigator - Third Officer	*A.P.Knowles* *J.Carpenter* *W.M.French* *R.S.M.Kyle*	*Captain* *Captain* *Navigator - 1st* *Third Officer*	*Collect by taxi at 6.30a.m.*
Cabin Crew - Purser - Main Steward(ess) - Steward(ess) - Steward(ess) - Steward(ess) - Steward(ess)	*Patrick Rea* *Mary Briscoe* *F.Buckle* *S.First* *Mohammed Razaq*	*Senior Purser* *Mrs* *Ms* *Mr* *Mr*	
Special Crew - Trainee Steward	*A.M.Learner*	*Mr*	*Completed training course last week*

On special trips, for example, long-haul routes, it may be necessary to modify this crew membership for that route, and obviously additional crew above the minimum may be allocated to any flight for any reason.

To conclude this example, the resultant model should enable us to see the workload of crew members and any flights they have taken as crew or passengers, and help Atlantis Island Flights ensure that all their crews are not overworked in their safety critical role.

Model the Open Ticket

If you look at the open ticket, you will notice that the only real difference is that there is no date quoted. It still refers to a passenger and a flight number. We therefore have tickets that can either be for a specific flight (on a date) or simply be open for a particular airline route. Remember it is the coupon that is really open not the ticket, which is a common misuse of terminology.

Figure 6-3
Using an Exclusive Arc for an Either/Or Situation

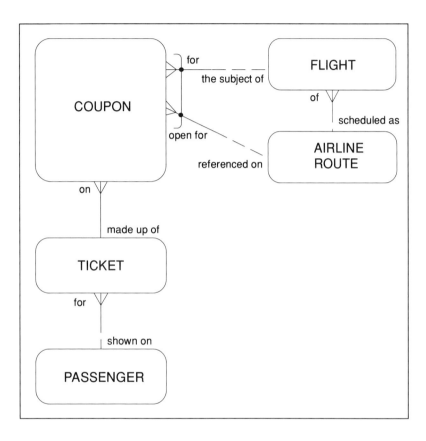

As in the credit card example we have used an exclusive relationship, shown by the arc. The diagram may now be read as follows:

Each COUPON must be either for one and only one FLIGHT or open for one and only one AIRLINE ROUTE.

Sub-typing

Flights could be of two different types, which we can show diagrammatically as follows.

Figure 6-4
Entity Sub-types

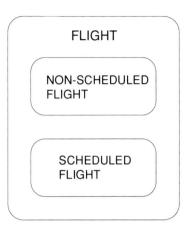

The inner boxes are called sub-types, and they must be mutually exclusive. They may have attributes and relationships of their own, but automatically inherit those of the outer box, which is called a super-type.

In our example we will guess, and later confirm with the user, that non-scheduled flights may be between any two airports and that we are only interested in the origin and final destination. Scheduled flights, however, conform to the origin and destination airports of the standard airline route. Thus we get the following structure.

Figure 6-5
Adding Relationships between
Sub-types and other Entities

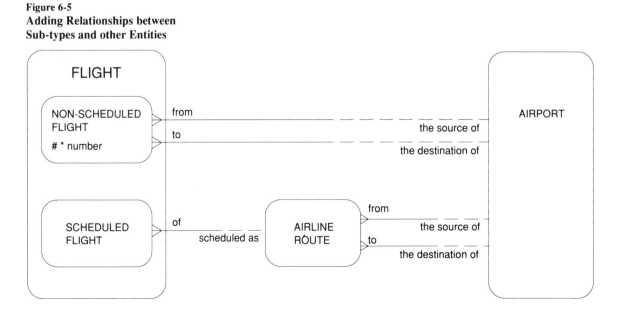

You will notice that this model does not allow a non-scheduled flight to be assigned to a preset airline route, identified by a standard flight number. Thus non-scheduled flights would need their own unique flight numbers (or the model is definitively wrong!).

Special Tickets

The actual tickets, or coupons, need little extra information to cater for the special aspects. Additional attributes on the ticket would give us:

TICKET   date of issue
             full fare
             discount given
             currency
             staff indicator.

Notice that we have put in the full fare applicable, which may vary by source and the discount given from which we can easily calculate the actual price paid. This then enables us to analyze discount levels, fares quoted by different issuing organizations and also correlate this with the real revenue. Later we might replace or add another attribute for discount reasons to help management find where all the lost revenue is going.

But how do we know whether the passenger was a crew member and what their workload is?

Well, we have to dispense with the concept of passengers! That is, as an entity on our diagram. Instead we must recognize that crew members, agents, captains, stewards, and so on, are all different roles or jobs of a person, and that a person is a passenger (or potential passenger) only by virtue of having either a booking, ticket or boarding pass. Thus the passenger concept disappears and is replaced by a set of relationships to an entity called PERSON, as shown in the next diagram.

Figure 6-6
Relationships to the
Entity PERSON

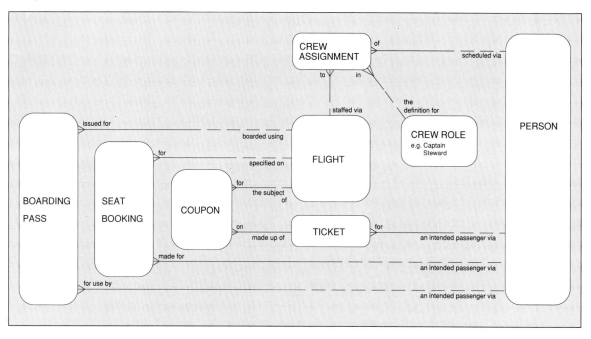

Notice that coupon, seat booking and boarding pass are not directly related, but all have relationships to both person and flight. Given this information, a computer or a person could easily match the data for a specified flight to find people who:

- had coupons but had no boarding pass, perhaps to ask them to check in.

- had seat bookings but no coupon, to ensure they buy a ticket before a boarding pass is issued.

- to work out what level of overbooking is practicable.

This method of modelling control information is common and shows up on a well-drawn diagram as a series of similar parallel relationships.

The crew assignment of person to flight, and its history, enables us to identify for any person not only their ticketed flights but also their flights by virtue of being on the crew. We could also examine this information and the related crew roles to see whether it looks sensible, but if we need the minimum standards for the aircraft or route, and for that matter the normal crew membership, we need the following additional components.

Figure 6-7
Standard Aircraft Crews

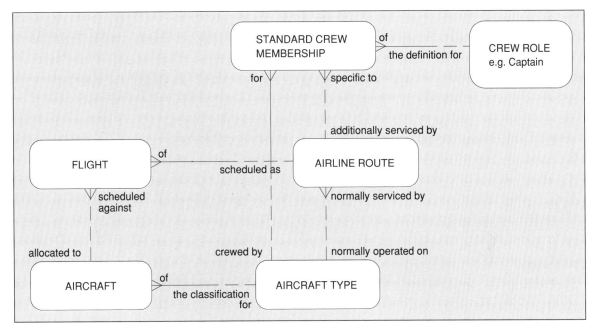

To assign people to make up a crew for an aircraft we need to know the normal or standard membership and the roles that must be included, such as a captain.

To find out the standard crew membership for a flight, we first need to know the aircraft that is to be used and thus the aircraft type as well as the airline route. One of two situations will then occur.

1. We can use the aircraft type to determine what standard crew membership is needed.

   Each AIRCRAFT TYPE may be crewed by one or more STANDARD CREW MEMBERSHIPs, each of which is of a defined CREW ROLE; for example, five memberships of the crew role steward(ess).

2. If the airline route has any special requirements for crew membership, perhaps because of excessive distance, then these would be additional to the standard crew membership by virtue of aircraft type.

An implementation of these relationships was shown earlier in this chapter, by the preprinted part of the Crew Roster.

The diagram overleaf adds the CREW ASSIGNMENT entity back, which now allows us to model all the data on the crew roster.

Figure 6-8
Matching Assignment to Standard

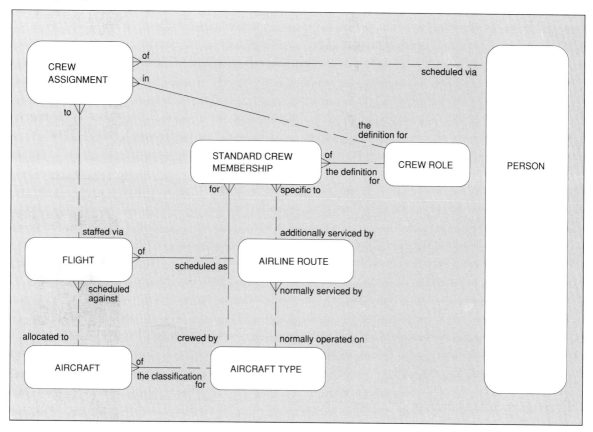

Function Example

Let us use the diagram to help define a business function:

Create crew assignments to the flight of people in specific crew roles based on both any standard crew membership requirements of crew roles for the aircraft type, which is the classification for the aircraft used for the flight, plus any other standard crew memberships specific to the airline route covered by the flight.

This function has been read straight off the diagram with a few 'noise' words added, and may need the words refining a little before it is set in front of users.

Notice, however, that the majority of the words used in the statement are derived from the diagram. This is most easily achieved when the relationship names are passive, having conformed to the rule that link phrases have to follow the verb **to be** (either must be or may be).

Standard Crews

Crew members may well be grouped together into a named crew, which whenever possible flies together. In which case, the above function would need to be extended to attempt to create the crew assignment out of a normal crew. The following extension to the model shows the information required, and introduces a new concept called non-transferable relationships, shown by a 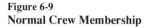 symbol.

Figure 6-9
Normal Crew Membership

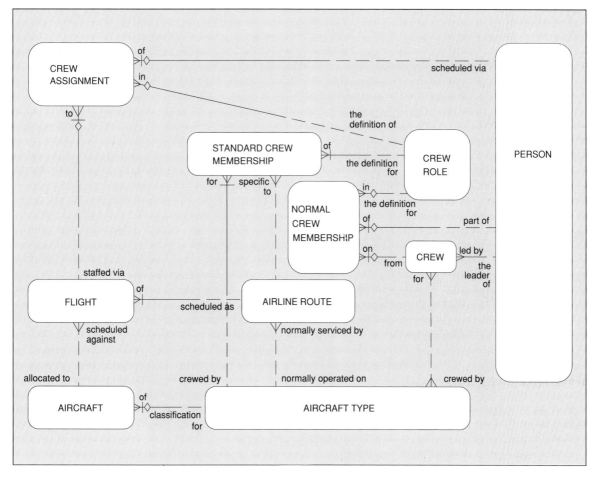

Notice that the diagram now shows us the list of crews that would normally be applicable for an aircraft type. (Many to many between CREW and AIRCRAFT TYPE.) From there, one can easily ascertain the normal crew membership of people on that crew, in their different roles.

Non-transferable Relationships

Many of the relationships have been defined as non-transferable, which means that once connected they cannot be reconnected to other instances of the reference entity. This is signified on the diagram by a small sign $\Diamond$ on the end of the relationship.

The attributes of NORMAL CREW MEMBERSHIP reflect this, as they are:

- date joined
- date left
- special duties.

Thus if someone changes their membership, the 'date left' information would be recorded and a new instance of their membership, perhaps with a different crew and/or role, would be created. This might reflect a promotion and a move to another crew, whilst maintaining a history of old crew members. If we had a large turnover, this information could be used to identify the situation and the person who was leader of the crew during that period.

Similarly, the history of crew assignments is important, so all its relationships are shown as non-transferable.

User Presentation

These models may get very complex and thus incomprehensible to the untrained eye. Whenever you present to end users, always provide them with a subset diagram that encompasses their area of knowledge and that immediately surrounding it.

When first presenting to them, build up a picture in small pieces until they see the whole. During these chapters we have introduced new concepts and additions to the model in small increments, discussed each and then moved on. In many cases we have deliberately missed off information previously covered (and agreed) to help us concentrate on a new topic. Do this with your users – they will appreciate it, enjoy the experience and help you get the model accurate more quickly.

So What Have We Found?

In this chapter we have found that for real requirements the basic set of rules was insufficient. We needed to add the concepts of:

- exclusive relationships
- entity sub-typing and
- non-transferable relationships.

This set of modelling conventions gives us a rich repertoire of techniques, which may be used to model any situation.

However, we need to understand these conventions thoroughly, as described in detail in Chapters 3 and 7. Many readers will find the appendices on data normalization, valid relationships and business views useful at this time. Why not read through those sections, finishing with Appendix G on business views and then re-read this chapter. (Try validating the model by creating business views for crew assignment and boarding pass.)

But there are some other chapters! They cover some recurring themes in entity relationship modelling and bring together many of the issues that are needed to produce a high quality model.

Remember, a high quality entity relationship model is one that is definitive, understandable by users and development staff alike, meets the needs of the business and supports all the relevant business functions. Given that, one can then go on to database and file design (Appendix F) with confidence.

7

ADVANCED CONVENTIONS AND DEFINITIONS

The earlier chapter on basic conventions should be read and fully digested before these advanced concepts are considered. As with any modelling technique there is no one definitive answer – otherwise, all cars from every manufacturer would be identical. Instead we have alternative models, architectures and designs, each of which must more than adequately meet the needs but offer different opportunities and compromises. Each alternative must, however, be rigorous and conform to the various guidelines laid down.

This chapter covers the concepts of:

Entity	sub-types
	super-types
	distinguishing between sub-types
	overlapping sub-types
	reference and intersection entities
	definition
	volumes over time
	distributed requirement
Relationship	resolution of many to many
	exclusivity
	non-transferable
	qualified degree
	definition
	redundancy
	useful names
	cascade delete (and update)

And also the concepts of:

Unique Identifier	by arc
Domain	definition detail and usage
Attribute	definition derived

Entity

Sub-type

An entity sub-type is a type of entity.

Sub-type Rules

An entity may be split into two or more mutually exclusive sub-types, each of which has common attributes and/or relationships. These common attributes and/or relationships are defined explicitly once only at the higher level. Sub-types may have both attributes and/or relationships in their own right. A sub-type may be further sub-typed to lower levels, and so on, but experience has shown that two or three levels cater for all but the most unusual circumstances.

A sub-type entity implicitly inherits all the attributes, relationships and business functions of the entity at the higher level, known as a super-type.

Super-type

A means of classifying an entity that has sub-types. An entity may well be both a sub-type of another entity and a super-type in its own right.

The sub-types for an entity must comprise a complete set. That is, all instances of the super-type must be classifiable as being one of its sub-types. In many cases this will involve adding an extra sub-type, called OTHER ENTITY, for completeness.

Both sub-type and super-type entities must conform to all the rules for an entity, as that is what they are.

Figure 7-1
The Super-type AIRCRAFT

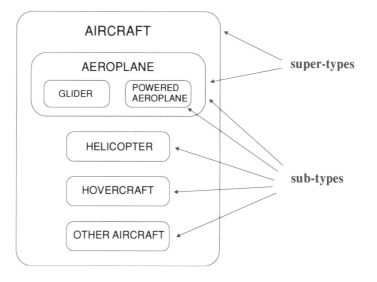

Notice that we have added a sub-type called OTHER AIRCRAFT, in case the others we have defined do not comprise the complete set of possible AIRCRAFT we may need to know about. A question, such as, *"What other types of aircraft do we need to know about?"* may help you identify missing sub-types or enable you to remove this 'OTHER' sub-type.

Syntax

When reading the name of a super-type one can add *"which must be either an A, B, C or D"*

> *... AIRCRAFT, which must be either an AEROPLANE, HELICOPTER, HOVERCRAFT or OTHER AIRCRAFT, ...*

When reading the name of a sub-type add *"which is a type of ..."*

> *... HELICOPTER, which is a type of AIRCRAFT, ...*

When both situations apply, do both!

> *... AEROPLANE, which is a type of AIRCRAFT and must be either a GLIDER or a POWERED AEROPLANE, ...*

Sub-type Quality Check

If a sub-type has no attributes, relationships or specially associated business functions, what is it? Perhaps it is just the synonym for something else.

Inverted Syntax

Simply turn the assertion around, for example:

> *... that means that an aeroplane is a type of aircraft in all cases and can never be classified other than as a glider or powered aeroplane. Is that true?*

Distinguishing Between Sub-types	When subsequently implementing a sub-type, one needs to have some method for differentiating between one sub-type and another. Three typical methods exist.

When subsequently implementing a sub-type, one needs to have some method for differentiating between one sub-type and another. Three typical methods exist.

1. At the implementation level add a new data item to which one gives allowable values for each of the possible sub-types. For example, the data item might be called ENTITY SUB-TYPE (e.g. AIRCRAFT SUB-TYPE).

2. At the business level, you can have an attribute that serves the same purpose. For example, an attribute called sex with the values male and female will give us two sub-types of PERSON.

3. Once more at the business level, you can have a combination of attributes/relationships and conditions on their values which define sub-types.

   For example, the entity ORDER could have the following sub-types:

Sub-type	Defining Conditions and/or Values
PENDING ORDER	where confirmed indicator = no
CONFIRMED ORDER	where confirmed indicator = yes AND completed date not known or later than today
COMPLETED ORDER	where completed date known AND = today or previous to today

Overlapping Sub-types (Orthogonal Sub-types)

Occasionally it is convenient to have overlapping or orthogonal sub-types; that is, when one might subset entities in more than one way. This will tend to be necessary when an entity can play many roles; for example, entities such as PERSON or ORGANIZATION UNIT.

The rules are the same; except that each set of sub-types should be named, and within each set the rules for mutual exclusivity apply.

For example, two sets of sub-types of the entity PERSON are EMPLOYMENT TYPE and GENDER.

An instance of the entity PERSON is identifiable as being a CURRENT EMPLOYEE, based on the to and from dates of current employment. A PERSON is identifiable as being a CLIENT CONTACT if there is a relationship to the CLIENT ORGANIZATION UNIT that employs him/her. As we have overlapping sub-types it is convenient to give a name to each set of sub-types. In this example we have chosen the name EMPLOYMENT TYPE.

Figure 7-2
The EMPLOYEE Sub-type Set

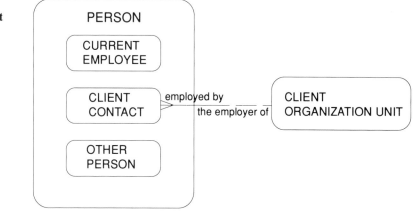

An instance of the entity PERSON is identifiable as being a MALE or FEMALE sub-type, based on the value of the attribute sex. For convenience, this set of sub-types is given the name GENDER.

Figure 7-3
The GENDER Sub-type Set

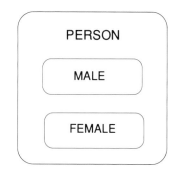

When overlapping sub-types occur, it is sensible to use, say, black to denote the most frequently-used sub-typing mechanism and other colours (as above) to denote other orthogonal sub-type sets.

Notice that the extra rules that can apply to sub-types are useful constraints to functions that create or update these entities – by reference in the function definition to the sub-type instead of the super-type.

The function definition *Create CLIENT CONTACT* implies that we have to supply all the attributes defined for the sub-type CLIENT CONTACT and all those attributes inherited from the entity PERSON. There is a further implication that we must create a relationship to a CLIENT ORGANIZATION UNIT, which is the employer of this CLIENT CONTACT. Further, a CLIENT CONTACT would not be given an attribute value for employment start date: this would only apply to the sub-type CURRENT EMPLOYEE.

Reference Entity

A reference entity is a useful term for an entity that has no mandatory relationship ends connected to it. (There are only a few such entities on a typical diagram.) It is also used to complete an accurate definition of other entities – this is where the reference entity is at the 'one' end of several many to one relationships.

'Type' entities such as AIRCRAFT TYPE are often reference entities, as are entities like ORGANIZATION UNIT and PERSON. One way of looking at things is that instances of reference entities can exist in their own right, without reference to other things.

Intersection Entity

An intersection entity is one that resolves a many to many relationship between two other entities. The instances of the resulting intersection entity can only exist in the context of the two reference entities as shown.

Figure 7-4
Reference and
Intersection Entities

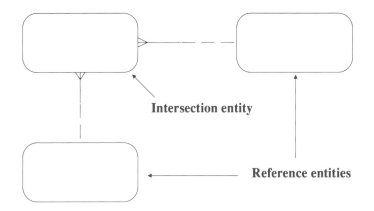

Intersection entity

Reference entities

Entity Definition

By the end of detailed analysis the information requirement represented by an entity may require each of the following:

- name
- plural
- synonyms
- volumes and possibly growth patterns
- description
- notes/remarks

and associated:

- attributes (at least two)
- relationships (at least one)
- unique identifier (at least one)
- usage by business functions (at least one).

A more complete definition is shown in Appendix C.

Distributed Requirements

In a decentralized organization the same entity may be used in different ways. In this case, the definition should include the volume of each entity by location or business unit.

Detailed Definition

A complete detailed definition, along with rules, is shown in Appendix C, which also includes the standard forms you would need to fill in.

Relationships

Resolution of Many to Many Relationships

Many to many relationships will be common during early strategy or analysis periods. By the end of the analysis stage they should all be resolved, unless they represent a simple two way list of information. Resolution is achieved by means of inserting a new intersection entity between the two ends as below.

Figure 7-5
Resolving a Many to Many Relationship with an Intersection Entity

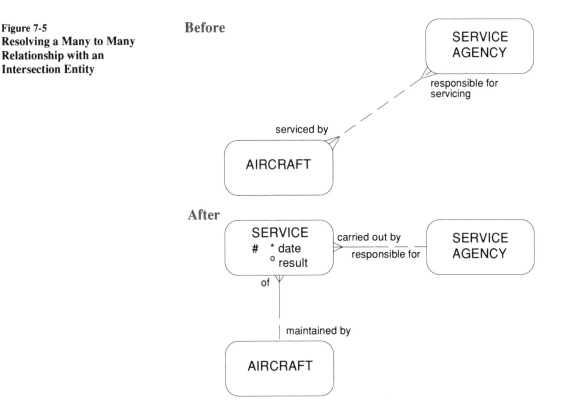

The newly created entity must be named; this is often suggested by establishing the noun from one of the original relationship names as above. As you can see the model now enables us to track services for aircraft. Then descriptive attributes, relationship to other entities and so on are added, as normal.

Exclusivity

Two or more relationships, from the same entity, may be mutually exclusive.

Representation

This is represented by an arc across each of the relevant relationship ends, with a small dot/circle where they join.

Figure 7-6
An Exclusive Arc

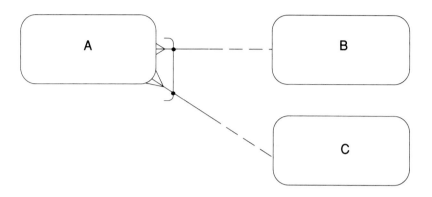

Where there is another relationship in between, the arc may cross it without a dot/circle.

Figure 7-7
The Same Exclusive Arc
Showing that the
Relationship between A and
D is Not Part of It

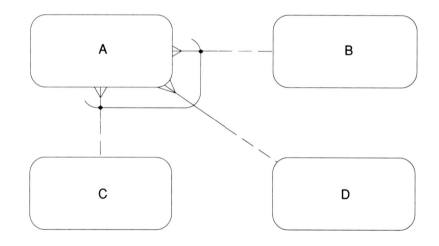

Alternatively, you may dispense with the dots and break the arc as shown in Figure 7-8.

Figure 7-8
A Different Way to Show
the Same Exclusive Arc

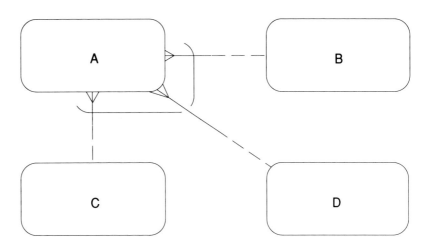

Where several arcs are used around a single entity, place them at different distances from the entity for clarity, as in Figure 7-9.

Rules

- Arcs may only span relationship ends that are either all mandatory or all optional.

- A relationship end can only be in one arc.

- An arc must span at least two relationship ends, and normally would not span more than three or four.

- Arcs are nearly always drawn across the many ends of relationships.

- Arcs may not span relationships from different entities, nor from sub-type entities and their super-types.

- If one relationship end that is part of the unique identifier is in an arc, then each of the other relationship ends within the arc must also be part of alternative unique identifiers for the entity.

Figure 7-9
Illustrating Some of the
Rules for Exclusive Arcs

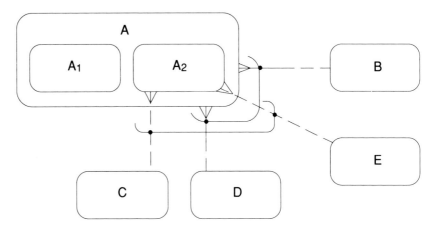

Syntax

The syntax for reading relationships now changes to include the words **either** and **or**, to unambiguously reflect the exclusivity, as below.

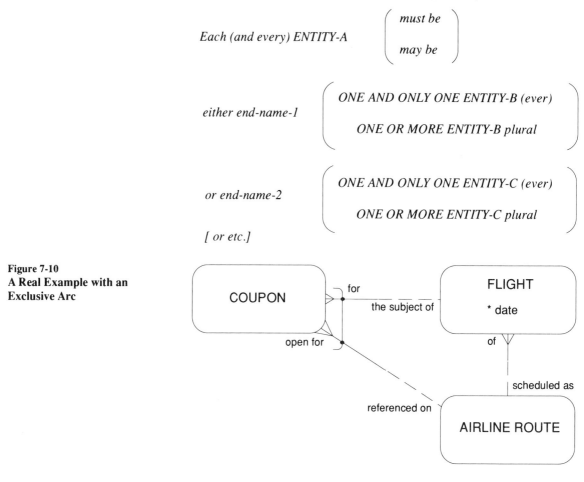

Each (and every) ENTITY-A

$\left(\begin{array}{c} \textit{must be} \\ \\ \textit{may be} \end{array} \right)$

either end-name-1

$\left(\begin{array}{c} \textit{ONE AND ONLY ONE ENTITY-B (ever)} \\ \\ \textit{ONE OR MORE ENTITY-B plural} \end{array} \right)$

or end-name-2

$\left(\begin{array}{c} \textit{ONE AND ONLY ONE ENTITY-C (ever)} \\ \\ \textit{ONE OR MORE ENTITY-C plural} \end{array} \right)$

[or etc.]

Figure 7-10
A Real Example with an
Exclusive Arc

Each COUPON must be either for one and only one FLIGHT (on a specific date) or open for one and only one AIRLINE ROUTE (identified by a flight number but no date, i.e. an open coupon/ticket).

Inverted Syntax

Once more, we may use inverted syntax as follows:

That means that we can never have any form of COUPON that is not for either a specific FLIGHT (on a date) or is open for (a quoted flight number of) a STANDARD FLIGHT. Is that true?

Notice that we used identifying attributes to help convey the information definitively.

Invalid Combinations

Figure 7-11
Arcs that Break Various
Rules

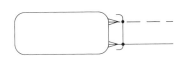

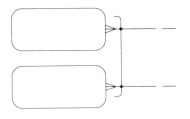

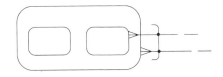

Each of the above fails logic checks.

Unusual arcs

Figure 7-12
An Arc Across the One
End of a Relationship

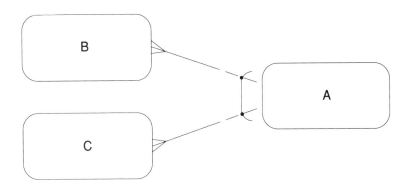

This means that A is often comprised of either a set of Bs or Cs, but never a combination.

(Beware: this usage is often employed to try to put in policy rules, which are liable to frequent change. Such rules are best addressed by some form of logic in a function that references a part of the entity relationship model that includes entities for rules and policy.)

Normally an entity instance may be connected to another via a relationship, and subsequently it may be disconnected and re-connected to another instance of the same type. If this is not allowed, then the relationship (end) is said to be non-transferable.

Representation

A non-transferable relationship is signified by a ◊ on the appropriate end.

**Figure 7-13
Example**

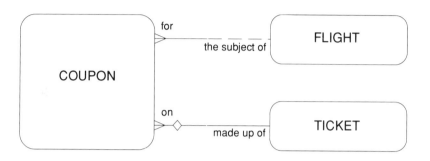

It would not make any sense to have a coupon transferred to become part of another ticket, but it would make sense to have the coupon switched to refer to a different flight; for example, because of overbooking. Note that the flight could be a later one with the same airline or even a switch to another airline, as has happened to me several times.

Syntax

One can add the clause *"and it can never be transferred"* to the standard means of reading relationships.

> *Each COUPON must be on one and only one TICKET, and it can never be transferred to another TICKET.*

Invert the syntax by asking whether the assertion is true in all cases.

Qualified Degree

Occasionally it is important to be able to define the limits of a degree, and the normal, maximum, average and 95 percentile usage. Subsequently, this information can be vital to designers.

Representation

Use the symbols $=, >, \geq, <, \leq$ as appropriate.

**Figure 7-14
Example 1**

Each YEAR may be made up of one and up to twelve MONTHs.

Figure 7-15
Example 2

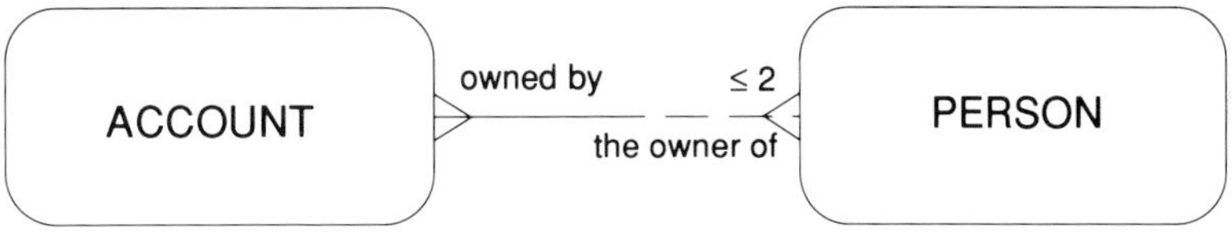

Each ACCOUNT must be owned by one and up to two PEOPLE.

(i.e. joint accounts are allowed.)

In rare cases it may be vital to draw a distribution graph to show usage, as illustrated by the following example.

Figure 7-16
Example 3

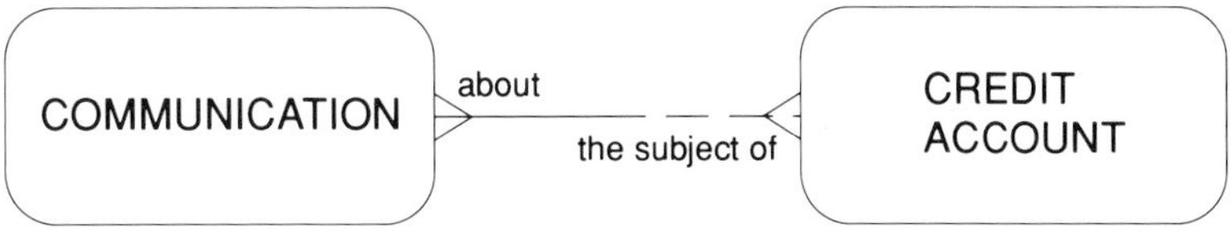

Figure 7-17
A Distribution Graph

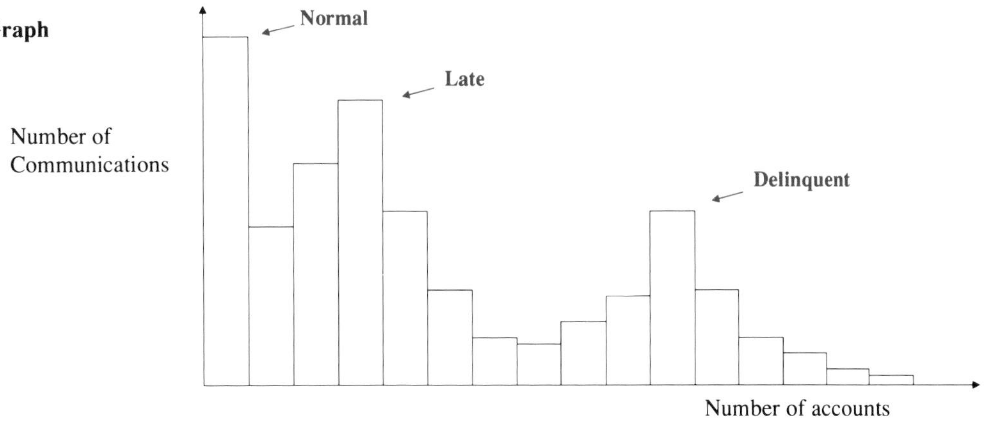

The peaks represent:

– normal accounts
– accounts that had late payments
– accounts that had gone 'delinquent'
  (i.e. fraud was suspected and letters were being sent everywhere to track the culprit).

This information for several million accounts makes a dramatic change to both the database design and that of the manual filing system storage technique.

Relationship Definition

By the end of detailed analysis the information requirement represented by a relationship may require each of the following for each end:

- degree
- name
- optionality (possibly qualified)
- notes

and associated:

- entities (exactly two)
- arcs (zero or one only)
- unique identifiers
- usage by business functions.

A more complete definition is shown in Appendices B and C. This also shows a set of useful relationship end names, in case you find it difficult at first to think of accurate and useful names.

Redundant Relationship

An Entity Relationship Diagram should not have any relationships that can, in **all** circumstances, be derived from other relationships.

Note: in a database, file or manual implementation of relationships redundancy is common to ensure performance. These must be design decisions and not be pre-empted (perhaps incorrectly) by the analyst.

Figure 7-18 Example

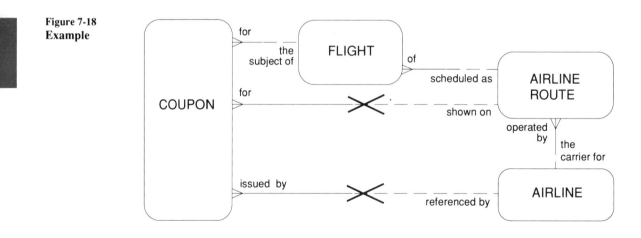

At first sight this diagram appears plausible and certainly reflects the data printed on some coupons; however, the relationship COUPON for FLIGHT unambiguously identifies both the AIRLINE ROUTE and AIRLINE, thus making the other two relationships from COUPON redundant.

Cascade Delete

In the real world, when we lose all knowledge of something we often implicitly lose all knowledge of some associated things.

> For example, if we delete all knowledge of a TICKET we implicitly delete all knowledge of its COUPONs. COUPONs (the children) only exist within the context of a TICKET (the parent entity).

This is known as 'cascade delete' and applies to some relationships as viewed from the many or child end.

In non-cascade delete situations, there is often an implicit rule that deletion would be inhibited for dependent entities (children).

> For example, one could not delete a CREW whilst it still had MEMBERS.

Cascade Delete Indicator

An indicator is used to show the Cascade Delete status.

> C = Delete all children if the parent is deleted.
> X = Inhibit deletion of parent if any children still exist.
> N = Deletion of parent and child can be performed separately.

The inhibit rule (X) normally only applies when the child **must be** associated with the parent.

The separate deletion option (N) normally applies when both ends of the relationship are optional.

Cascade Update

This only applies at the implementation level, and is included for information only when using a relational database management system (RDBMS). If the unique identifier/primary key of the parent changes, the new value is automatically used to replace the value(s) for any foreign keys to that primary key.

Cascade Delete and Update may well be enforced automatically by the RDBMS and/or application generators.

Unique Identifier

In Chapter 3 we learnt that unique identifiers may be any combination of attributes and/or relationship ends.

If you combine the concept of exclusive relationships with that of a relationship end being part of a unique identifier, it becomes apparent that all the relationship ends in that arc should also be components of alternative unique identifiers.

Arcs in Unique Identifiers

Thus the unique identifiers may be any combination of attributes, relationship ends or exclusive arcs (and thus all the relationship ends thereby implied).

Domain

Definition of Term

A set of business validation rules, format constraints and other properties that apply to a group of attributes.

For example:

- a list of values
- a range
- a qualified list or range
- any combination of these.

Attributes in the same domain are subject to a common set of validation constraints. A more complete definition is given in Appendix C.

Usage

It is sensible to set up domain definitions for commonly recurring attributes such as:

- address line
- postal code/ZIP code
- grade (often with a list of values)
- salary (may be constrained by a range of allowable values).

Representation

It is not normal to represent domains on a diagram. When attributes are displayed on a diagram it may occasionally be useful to colour code or otherwise highlight those in a given domain.

Example

A company may well wish to standardize on name and address details for companies, people, locations, and so on. Thus each address would be composed of similar attributes, each of which was constrained to identical domain constraints.

	Domain
Address line-1	Address
Address line-2	Address
Address line-3	Address
Town (or City)	Address
County (or State)	Address
Country	Address
Post code (or ZIP code)	Postal code

Where Address is a maximum 32 character domain and Postal code is a domain with the country's validation rules defined.

Notice that this definition, with number attributes, conflicts with the appendix on data normalization, but it is normally a highly practical business (and implementation) model. On occasions a 'one to many' relationship to a concept called ADDRESS LINE with text description, sequence and type is applicable.

Attribute

The accurate definition of attributes is probably second equal in importance to that of relationships. When implemented on paper, database or other media, these become the primary data content that everyone in the world spends their time creating, changing, manipulating and reporting on. Entities and domains are, in many ways, just the labels and categories to help us group and control attributes.

Definition

Any detail that serves to qualify, identify, quantify or express the state of an entity
or
Any description of a 'thing of significance'.

Usage

By the nature of the definition of the term entity, every entity should have at least two attributes by the end of detailed analysis to record the information that needs to be known about it, and one is normally required during the strategy stage to aid understanding.

Finding attributes that form part or all of unique identifiers is important early on, and mandatory before design may commence. On occasion it is sensible, from a business point of view, to create 'system-generated' unique identifiers (such as employment number) to complement the sometimes unknown but preferred identifying attributes.

Representation

On an Entity Relationship Diagram the character before the attribute name signifies its cardinality:

* attribute-name		mandatory
° attribute-name		optional
#	* attribute-name	mandatory and part of the primary unique identifier.

Attributes need not be put on diagrams, unless required to aid understanding.

Attribute Properties

The important properties for an attribute are its name, description, format and length. Attributes are not always data. As with domains, an attribute may have values that are constrained by some rules. The simplest is conformance to a list of values; for example, the 'position' attribute on SEAT may be constrained to the values of aisle, window and centre.

By the end of detailed analysis the information requirement represented by an attribute may require each of the following to be defined:

- name
- description
- format
- length
- value(s) and/or a range of values

and associated:

- entity
- unique identifier(s)
- domain
- usage by business functions.

A full definition is covered in Appendix C.

Derived Attribute

Conceptually, these are attributes whose value is never set by a user or any other mechanism. The value is always derived at the instant in time it is required.

> For example, on our airline model we have a relationship between AIRCRAFT and its SEATs. A derived attribute that we could add to the entity AIRCRAFT might be named 'number of seats'. This attribute could be derived by 'count of SEATs on AIRCRAFT'.

> Another example would be to add a derived attribute called 'actual price paid' to the entity TICKET, with a derivation of 'full fare ...discount given'.

There are dangers with this derived attribute concept which must be understood before it is used in database design.

Obviously, each time there is a change in the value of any of the attributes from which we get a derived attribute the value of the derived attribute itself will also change. Depending on how the database is designed, this new value may be calculated either each time the derived attribute is used or each time its value actually changes.

In Appendix F on database design, all attributes become columns or data items. Do we **really** want that, as it would result in the value of a derived attribute being re-calculated each time a change occurs in any of the attributes from which it is derived? This represents a potentially high overhead in performance and increased space utilization. Perhaps it would be more effective to calculate its value only when it is actually needed.

On the other hand, if the value of a derived attribute changes only rarely but the attribute is used by many functions, to re-calculate the attribute value each time it is needed would also represent a high performance overhead. Calculating the value when it changes would greatly reduce the processing in this situation.

Recognizing these two opposing design issues, and ensuring that your analysts and designers understand each other clearly in this respect allows the analyst to use this powerful concept of derived attributes for entities (and business view – see Appendix G). When defining business functions, the analyst can then quote derived attributes in conditions to simplify the complexity of function logic.

For example:

> *"Identify any ticket where the actual price paid is less than half the full fare"*

as opposed to:

> *"Identify any ticket where the full fare minus discount given is less than half the full fare"*

Other Possible Attribute Properties

Remember that for most practical use we are interested in some form of computerized and/or manual data processing, such that formats of character, number, date, and so on, will be prevalent. However, this is not always the case, and the following may well be important on occasions:

- photograph
- fingerprint   - perhaps as a unique identifier
- sound   - for an impression of someone
- colour
- spectrograph value
- smell
- taste
- image
- video
- pulse
- and so on.

Often these are required for integration of computer and other systems – sometimes because computerization is not required.

Naming

Any attribute name must be simple and singular, and must not contain the name of the entity. Subsequently, one may qualify the attribute name in one of two ways to avoid ambiguity:

entity name attributen ame
or
attribute name of entity name

Figure 7-19
Example

The attribute name is simply 'date', as it is always in the context of the entity FLIGHT. In a function description it may be referred to in either of the above ways, such as:

"check date of flight" or *"check flight date"*.

Summary

We have found some very useful additional conventions and definitions, in particular those of:

- sub-types and super-types
- exclusive relationships
- non-transferable relationships.

These concepts not only give us a richer set of modelling techniques to accurately represent our understanding of the business, they **also** give our implementors rules that implicitly must be included in any clerical or computer implementation.

With CASE tools, many or all of these rules will be automatically enforced by the RDBMS or application generators. It can therefore pay high dividends to **get it right early**

8

CLASSICAL STRUCTURES AND GENERIC PATTERNS

This chapter contains several commonly found structures, which may prove useful as templates for use in your organization. Please assume that they are definitively wrong for your business, but will give you guidance on the shape, structure and quality to aim for.

The first set illustrates classical structures for:

- Hierarchies/organization units
- Networks
- Changes over time/history
- Bill of materials
- Classification and categories
- Entity types.

The second set illustrates specific examples, which may have applicability in many cases.

Example	Also applicable to
Orders	Contracts, agreements, delivery documents, invoices, credit notes, etc.
Roles and jobs	Client contact, organization unit
Products	Equipment, components, parts
Management information	Budgets, forecasts, actuals

The chapter concludes by illustrating how generic entity relationship models may be produced.

Classical Structures
Hierarchies

Modelling hierarchies can be complex in certain circumstances, but there are several generic patterns that cover most circumstances. The following example uses organization units.

Figure 8-1
A Hierarchic
Organization Structure

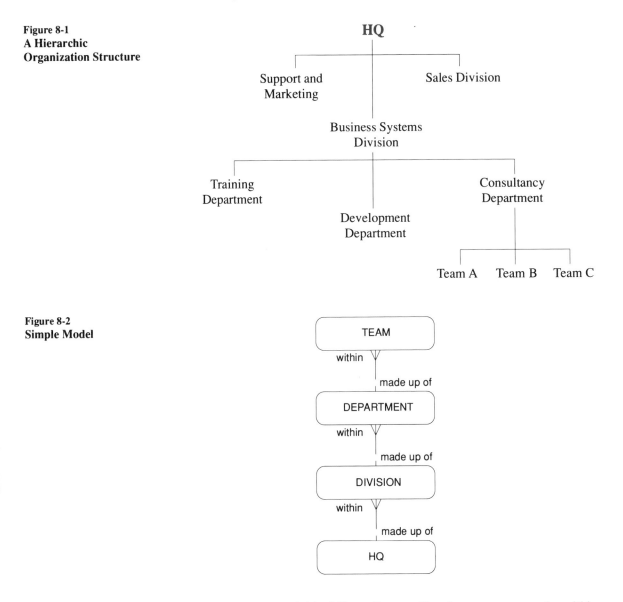

Figure 8-2
Simple Model

This simple model is OK, until we realize that teams cannot be within divisions, departments cannot report directly to companies, and only the four terms Team, Department, Division and HQ can be allowed. Also, what happens if we introduce another level?

Figure 8-3
Alternative 1

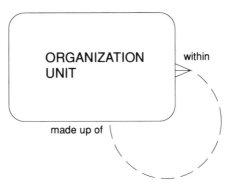

This model is useful, but there is no differentiation between the top of a hierarchy or any other node.

Figure 8-4
Alternative 2

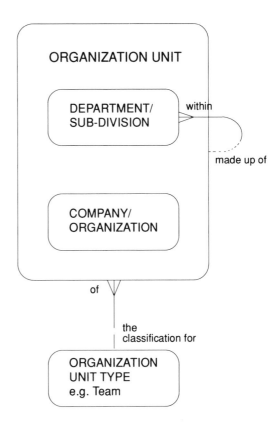

This is very useful, as it again caters for any number of levels. Each level must be of a defined type that allows many alternative names for levels. Separating the tops of the hierarchies (COMPANY) enables us to have separate relationships and functions that only apply to them.

Figure 8-5
Alternative 3

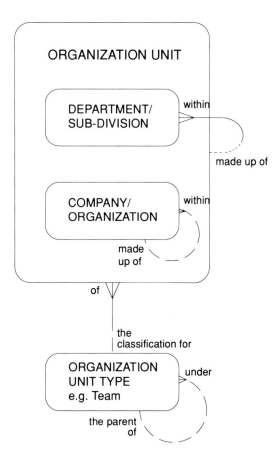

This extension recognizes that there are sometimes companies within company structures, which need modelling for financial analysis purposes. The relationship around organization unit type enables us to model the allowable rules of what type of unit may be under another type. These rules are restricted to a never changing structure.

Change Over Time

But things do change.

Companies get reorganized.

We still may need to analyze by the organization unit in its own right, within current organization roll-up or within previous roll-ups.

Thus we need a network instead, starting from the following model.

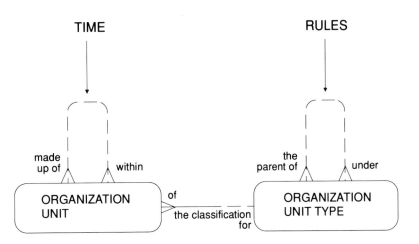

Figure 8-6
Allowing for Changes
Over Time

TIME   RULES

This leads us to a highly generic alternative, which will cater for most exceptional requirements.

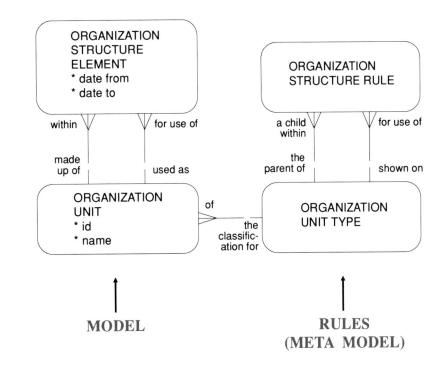

Figure 8-7
Alternative 4
Generic Model

MODEL   RULES
(META MODEL)

This has one major drawback – in 99% of cases business functions tend to deal with the **current** structure, not the intended or historic.

Let us therefore be practical and model it in a hybrid of the alternatives 3 and 4 above.

Figure 8-8
Alternative 5

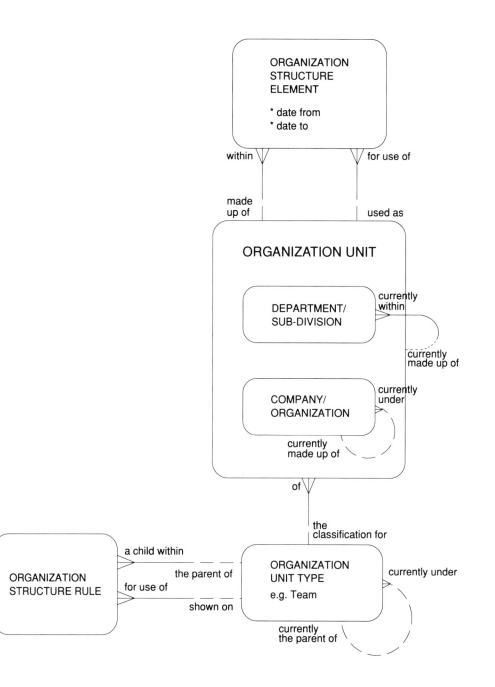

Now the structure element entities can be used for the complex but rare cases and the centre of the model for the normal situations.

This is actually a design concept of such significance that it is worth establishing the need at the business analysis level.

Networks

Figure 8-9
A Network Structure

A network structure is very common in Entity Relationship Diagrams.

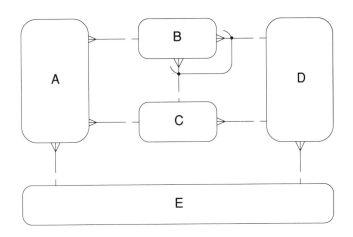

Here we have a structure with many hierarchies:

- E/D/B/A
- E/D/C/A
- E/D/C/B/A
- E/A

Each of these enables us to associate entities E and A in a complex network, thus one could follow the path shown with instances of these entities. From an E find all associated As directly; for each find the associated C and thus an instance of a D and E.

Step 1	start at an E
Step 2	select all directly associated As
Step 3	for each A, select the associated C and its associated D and its associated E (from which point you may restart at step 1)
Step 4	also for each A select the associated B for which either select its associated D and its associated E (another restart point)
Step 5	or select its associated C and its associated D and its associated E (for a final restart point)

Figure 8-10
Simple Network Example

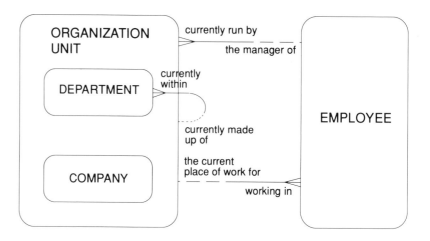

In this example, one may start at an employee and find the organization unit in which the employee is currently employed, and thus find the employee who is currently the manager of that unit.

If the organization unit is a department, one can find which organization unit it is currently within and thus its manager (and so on up the organization hierarchy). Obviously one can use this network to find who works in which department in all cases.

Note: the model is definitively incorrect in most circumstances as it does not allow an employee to work in more than one department; it does not cater for time; joint managers/directors are not allowed for either companies or departments; and so on.

We also have an interesting point of logic, as an instance of an organization unit cannot exist without there being an employee to be the manager of it! And conversely, an instance of an employee cannot exist without there being an organization unit which is his or her current place of work. A chicken and egg situation – which comes first?

You should now have the skills to improve this model.

Changes Over Time
(History and future)

The nature of an attribute may change over time; for example, the state of a contract. When considering time, we may find values for attributes which are held by an instance of an entity during overlapping time periods; for example, the names or pseudonyms of a person. A relationship may, over time, be associated with a different instance of an entity; for example, the home of a person.

Each of these is catered for in the same manner; that is, by creating a new entity associated to the first and assigning it values for the time period in question.

Attribute Changes

Figure 8-11
The Attribute status
Becomes an Entity

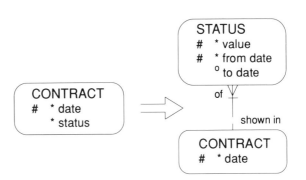

Consideration of the unique identifier of STATUS generates several business questions; for example,

"May a contract ever be in more than one state on the same day?"

Figure 8-12
The Attribute surname
Becomes an Entity

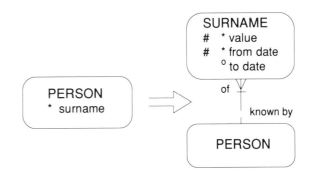

This model now enables us to hold information about all a person's different names, even allowing for different names at the same time. Notice that there is nothing to stop you holding an intended surname, perhaps because of an intended marriage.

'As it stands, the model even allows you to revert to an earlier name at a later date in your life.'

Relationship Changes

Figure 8-13
Adding a New Entity to Cater for a
Relationship Change

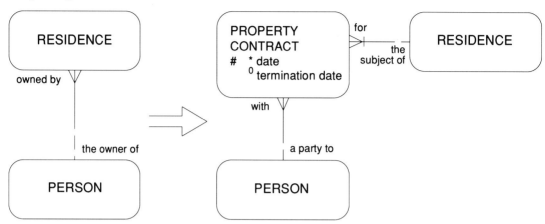

The new model enables a person to have property contracts for more than one residence concurrently and overlapping over a period of time. Similarly, the owner's residence can be ascertained via the contract. Note the model only allows for a single owner – perhaps you can change that.

Bill of Materials
(Implosion/explosion)

In most manufacturing organizations a bill of materials structure is essential to help identify:

- which parts are used in different products and
- what products and parts are made of.

In these cases, we are talking about **types** of parts and products. The same type of part (e.g. a motor) may be used as a component in many other parts or products. This is shown by the simple diagram below.

Figure 8-14

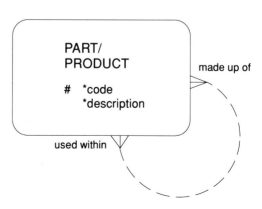

This model, however, is insufficient as we need to know **how many** and perhaps **what the fitting instructions are**. We achieve this by creating an intersection entity for these attributes (as we always do for a many to many relationship).

Figure 8-15
Creating an Intersection Entity
to Resolve a Many to Many
Relationship

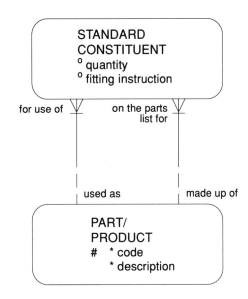

Parts Explosion

Each PART or PRODUCT may be made up of one or more STANDARD CONSTITUENTS, with their quantity and fitting instructions, each of which must be for the use of a different PART or PRODUCT.

Used in List

Conversely, each PART or PRODUCT may be used as one or more STANDARD CONSTITUENTS, each of which must be on the parts list for another PART or PRODUCT.

There is a problem with this diagram with the words. You must assume the shape is correct but that the words probably need to be changed to meet the naming conventions of the organization being modelled. As you go from company to company the following words can be interchanged in their meaning. You must determine the appropriate ones for your context:

- – Part
- – Component
- – Constituent
- – Product
- – Parts list item
- – Equipment
- – Plant
- – and many others!

Classifications and Categories

We all love to give things labels. Unfortunately we rarely give them mutually exclusive labels and rarely classify things in only one way. **Flexible systems** often require that key entities may be classified in as many ways as required from time to time by the business, including re-classifying that classification. How can we do this generically?

Figure 8-16
Simple Classification

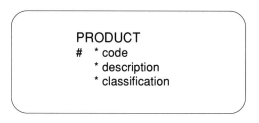

In this case we have used a simple attribute. Any classification value may be used to classify the product; there is no validation and each classification is assumed to be mutually exclusive. Each product can only be classified in one way at a time and the person who sets the classification must know what they mean.

Figure 8-17
Coded Classification

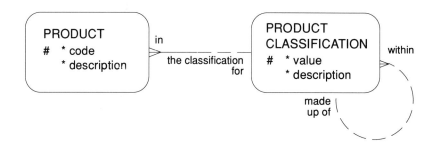

In this second case a preset product classification is required with a defined meaning or description; thus classifications are validated. However, a product may still be in one classification only at a time. We have also added a simple hierarchy of classifications to cater for different hierarchic sets of classifications.

Figure 8-18
Multiple Classifications

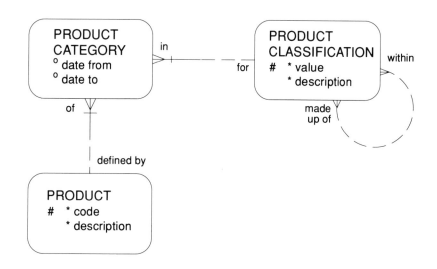

This model caters for a product being classified in as many ways as required at the same time. It also caters for multiple classifications over time. There is a many to many relationship around product classification to cater for multiple classifications of existing classifications.

Notice that this many to many relationship is a bill of materials structure, used in this case for classification.

Entity Types

There are several ways to define types of entity, which in part follow the same theme as the classifications mentioned above.

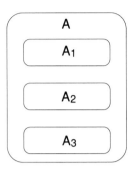

An entity A has three mutually exclusive sub-types A_1, A_2 and A_3. This is a highly constricted typing mechanism, as only three sub-types will ever be allowed, but it does allow us to define attributes and relationships which are specific to the sub-types.

Figure 8-20
Type Attribute

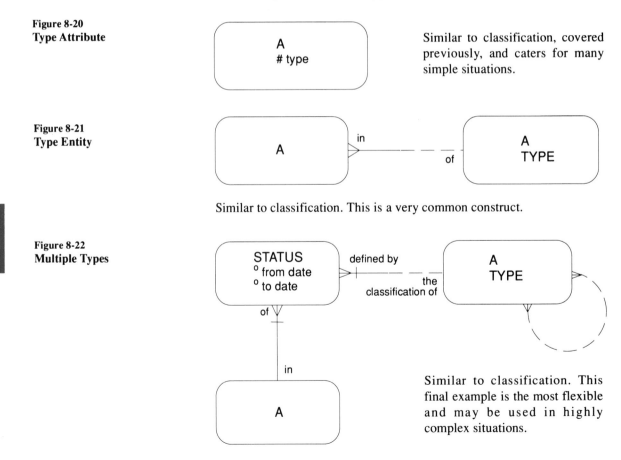

Similar to classification, covered previously, and caters for many simple situations.

Figure 8-21
Type Entity

Similar to classification. This is a very common construct.

Figure 8-22
Multiple Types

Similar to classification. This final example is the most flexible and may be used in highly complex situations.

Specific Examples

Orders

Figure 8-23
A Classical Structure for Orders

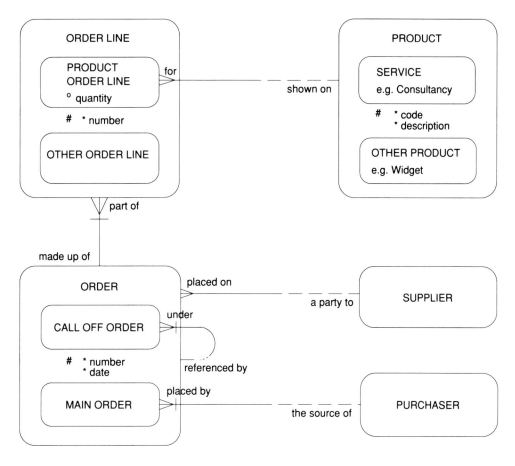

Notes:

In this diagram, products and services are assumed to be very similar.

The OTHER ORDER LINE sub-type is to move our thinking towards tax, delivery details, comments, terms and conditions, and so on, on an order.

The model allows tracking of an any-level hierarchy of orders within orders, which may be vital in a quality-tracking context.

Supplier and purchaser have been kept separate, which is normal for small businesses. For larger businesses, these would need to be combined to allow internal ordering.

In the case of internal ordering, some of the possible synonyms and examples are very interesting.

ORDER	Contract
	Agreement
	Licence
	Requisition
	Internal Order
MAIN ORDER	Main Contract
	Primary Contract
CALL OFF ORDER	Sub-contract
	Sub-order
Examples	Repairs and Maintenance Contract
	Service Agreement
	Fixed Price Contract
	Time and Materials Contract.

Other documents

Try replacing the word ORDER by DELIVERY (or INVOICE) throughout the above model. Some changes will be necessary, but the shape is fundamentally correct for many different types of control documents.

Roles and Jobs

A starting point might be a list of examples as follows:

Roles: client contact, buyer, inside salesman, first aider, project leader, lecturer, hacker.

Jobs: manager, clerk, sales executive, fitter, nurse, teacher, programmer.

Notes:

In the diagram opposite, types of role and job are kept distinct.

Job type could be extended to cover grading, payroll coding, full job descriptions, and so on. Here we have simply shown OBJECTIVES to distinguish them from roles. In a larger model, OBJECTIVES may need to be prefixed by an adjective to differentiate them from other objectives on the model.

It is assumed that EMPLOYMENT CONTRACT is only applicable to INTERNAL ORGANIZATION UNITs. Notice that by moving the relationship line to the super-type (ORGANIZATION UNIT) the model will then cater for tracking people through their various simultaneous, historic or intended employment.

In many countries, the word APPOINTMENT would be used instead of EMPLOYMENT CONTRACT; that is, people are appointed to a job (type), via a formal or informal contract of employment.

Figure 8-24
A Classical Structure for
Roles and Jobs

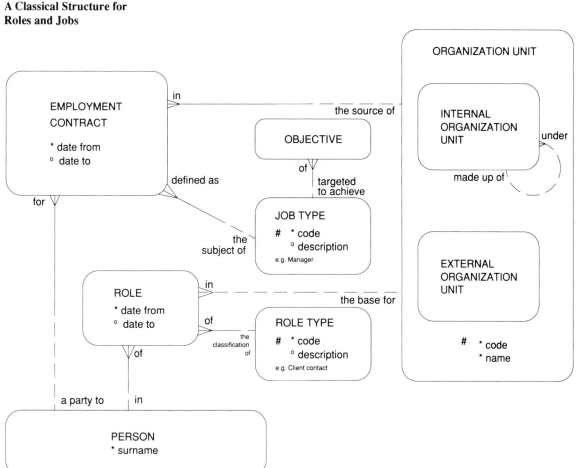

Products

If we combine some of the previous examples we get the following useful diagram for checking a new model for products.

Figure 8-25
A Classical Structure for
Products and Jobs

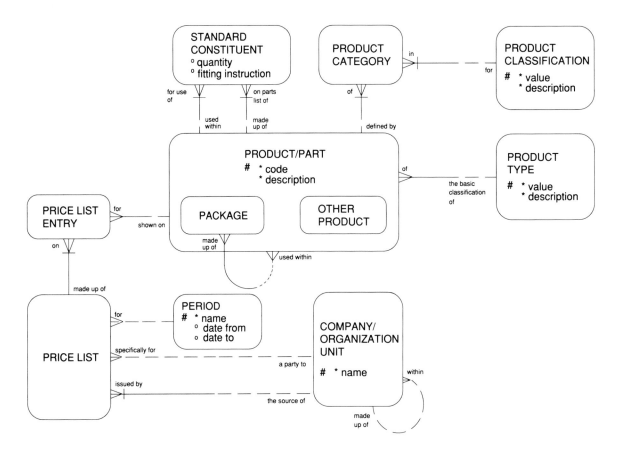

This example also caters for the marketing unit defining packages made up of other products (which themselves may be packages!).

Products tend to have different prices over a period of time, shown by the price list entry. This model also allows for a price list that has been specifically arranged for a company; and with the hierarchy around a company it also caters for the same list implicitly applying to all the lower organization units in the company.

Management Information	This example is to help us control the basic financial and resource information about some large project. The concept, however, may be used in many situations to control:

- Forecasts
- Budgets
- Actuals and
- Summary Actuals.

We will build up the picture to a final generic model.

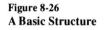Step 1

Consider a project with a simple set of forecasts, which possibly may be revised.

Figure 8-26
A Basic Structure

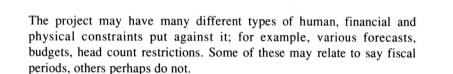

Step 2

The project may have many different types of human, financial and physical constraints put against it; for example, various forecasts, budgets, head count restrictions. Some of these may relate to say fiscal periods, others perhaps do not.

We could, therefore, use sub-types as below, but it may be difficult to predict all the possible sub-types we would ever need.

Figure 8-27
Adding Sub-types and the
Element of Time

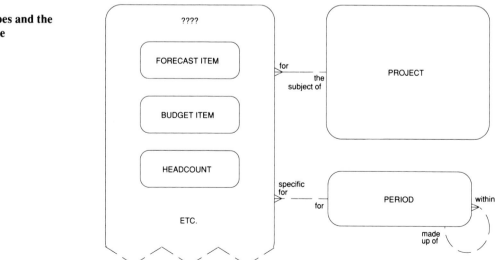

Step 3

Let us therefore create a generic entity called PROJECT PLAN ITEM and control it by means of PLAN TYPE, for which we may have as many instances as we need.

Figure 8-28
Using Further Entities to
Create a More Generic
Structure

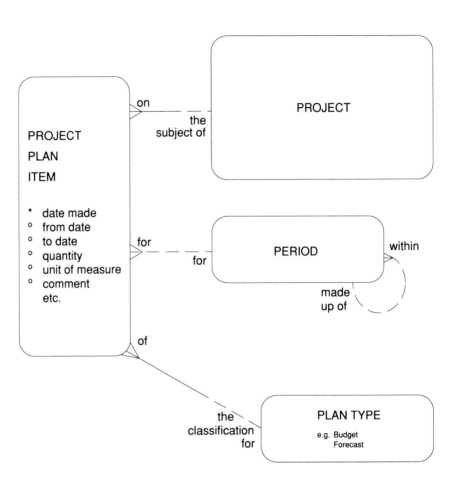

Step 4

To further classify forecasts, budgets, plans, and so on, we often quote the type of resource to be used. In rare cases we even mention a specific instance; for example, the use of a particular building or computer. The next diagram caters for this, using the word **rarely** to help us qualify the relationship.

Figure 8-29
Catering for Resources

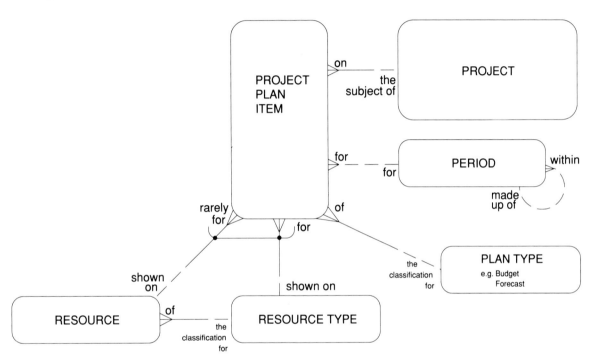

Step 5

Those were the plans, but what about recorded actual usage of resources?

We record these by various means such as timesheets for human resources, financial transactions and various mechanisms for physical resources (e.g. bookings for rooms). Once more these will often be for types of resources and occasionally for specific resources.

Figure 8-30
Using the Resources

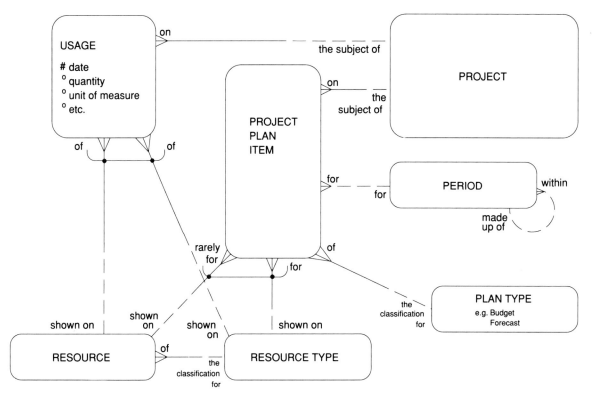

Step 6

When we create summaries of these actuals, normally for use within a particular period, the model becomes complex, as below.

Figure 8-31
The Extended Structure

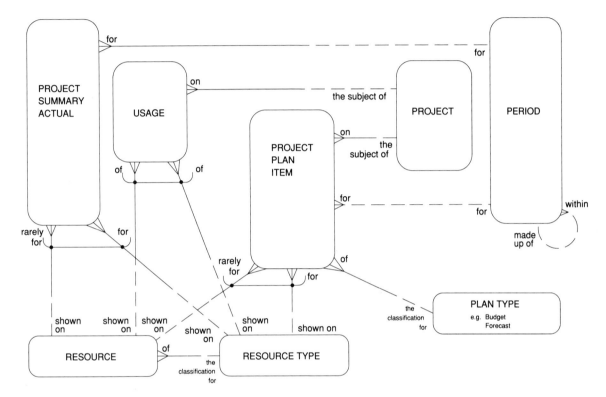

Step 7

The only sensible answer is to model this even more generically by recognizing the similarity of relationships and attributes between:

- Plan Item
- Usage and
- Summary Actual.

The following diagram is thus a very powerful model, which can be used to cater for management information under many circumstances. Try replacing the entity PROJECT with one for say TRAINING COURSE, ACCOUNT or PRODUCT DEVELOPMENT.

Figure 8-32
The Generic Model

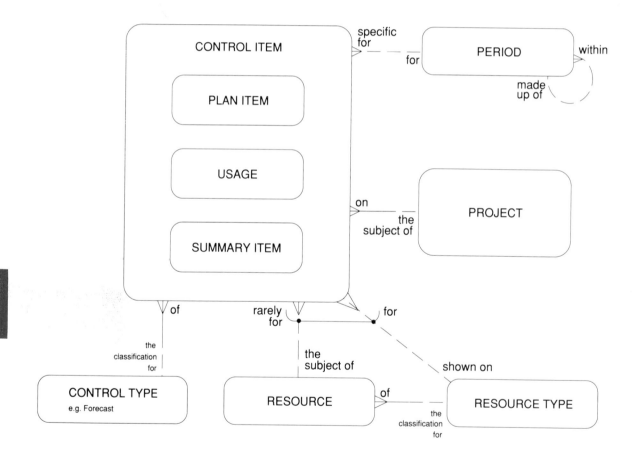

Generic Patterns

You will have seen from the last example that a simpler, more powerful model was produced by recognizing that many of the entities had similar attributes and/or relationships. You will often find that if you follow the layout rules given, such entities tend to migrate – this helps enormously when trying to find more generic structures.

Step 1

Identify possible opportunities for modelling more generically, for example:

Figure 8-33
A Basic Structure

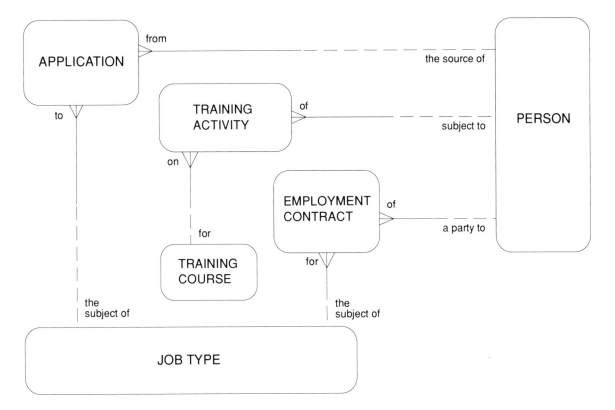

The three intersection entities all have similar attributes (mainly dates) and all have relationships to PERSON. If TRAINING COURSE and JOB TYPE were also considered to be similar we can go to Step 2.

Step 2

Figure 8-34
Two Generic Super-types
are Created

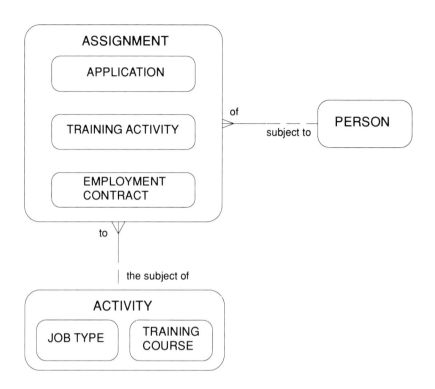

Now check it.

Can we still cater for all the circumstances the earlier model permitted?

Well yes we can, namely:

- applications for jobs
- training activities on courses
- employment contracts for jobs.

What else will it now cater for? How about:

- applications (or bookings?) for courses
- training activities on jobs (on-the-job training?)
- and even employment contracts for training courses (which is probably already catered for).

Finally look at the business functions, which should also be very similar. You may now be able to simplify them or create common functions that handle these new generic entities.

A Word of Warning

It is very easy to make models overly generic, as illustrated by the following model of 'life, the universe and everything'!

**Figure 8-35
The Ultimate in
Generic Models**

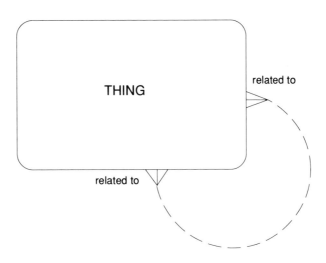

Always test out a new generic model with a colleague and your users.

These models are a communication vehicle and if you have overdone it you must step back to a less generic model, to keep the understanding of everyone involved.

Chapter

9

RELATED CONCEPTS

This book is primarily concerned with the concepts of entity, attribute, relationship and domain, and how they might be taken forward to a database or file design. There are other concepts that need consideration which are briefly covered in this chapter. They are:

- dataflow
- datastore
- business function
- business event
- schema architecture
- entity life-cycle.

Dataflow and Datastore

Many analysts and designers use the concept of a dataflow diagram, which enables business functions that are interrelated to be modelled by showing the data that flows into and out of them, as illustrated by the diagram on the next page.

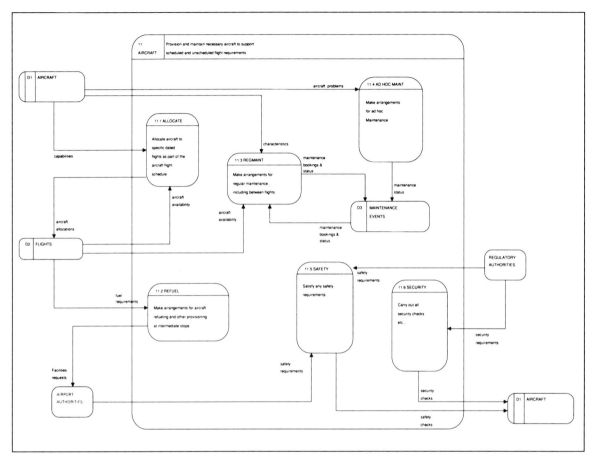

Each of the arrows → represents a named dataflow.

Each of the open-ended boxes represents a temporary or permanent datastore for logical data/attributes, as used by different business functions.

The definition of each dataflow and datastore is in terms of a set of constituent attributes of entities taken from the entity relationship model. In a few cases they will also contain derived data, such as 'profit', in which case they would normally be derivable from known attributes. This is an important completeness check.

The content of any datastore must reflect the union of any associated dataflows.

Business Function/Process
Any business function, particularly one that is elementary, should be a definition of **what** the business does, or needs to do, irrespective of **how** it is done. It should be defined as a sentence starting with a verb, which references entities or synonyms of entities and describes data changes and conditions in terms of attributes.

Business Event
Many business functions are triggered by various forms of events in the business. These can include real-time events (e.g. thirty days after invoice date), change events (when some details are changed or new information arrives in the business) or system events (when the conclusion of one or more business functions acts as the trigger for some other function to start).

Each of these events would be defined and may include a statement of the condition when it occurs. Such conditions should be defined in terms of known attributes.

Schema Architecture
One often hears about a three-schema architecture. With CASE*Method, the conceptual or business level model of information is represented by the entity relationship model. This may then be translated into a logical design, as illustrated in Appendix F. A logical design is typically a normalized relational database design, with no consideration given to access or space utilization.

The third form of schema is, therefore, when this logical design is mapped onto a physical implementation, which addresses such issues as performance indexes, data clustering, disk (or filing) space utilization.

External Schema
Recently, the concept of external schema has been discussed. This represents the perceived view of information from the context of a user in a particular role. In CASE*Method it is considered to be a subset of one or more business views, sufficient to meet the functional needs of the user's role. (See Appendix G.)

Entity Life-cycle

When we have an entity relationship model with, say, a hundred entities, it is a useful quality check to select about ten of the most important entities and consider their life-cycles. This may indicate missing attributes, relationships, entities and both events and business functions that act on these entities.

For example, the life-cycle of a PRODUCT may include the following:

- product conception
- product specification
- product design
- prototype
- test product
- build manufacturing plant for product
- manufacture instances of product
- market and sell product
- and so on.

During this process an entity called PRODUCT PROTOTYPE, which needs careful analysis, may be discovered.

Other Concepts

There are many other concepts that may require understanding before a complete system may be engineered. These are covered by other books and training classes.

Chapter

10

QUALITY AND COMPLETENESS CHECKS

Peer Group Check

When producing high quality models that meet the business needs there is no substitute to having well-trained analysts/designers who thoroughly understand the business and the full range of modelling techniques covered by this book.

We all need help, however, and that of our colleagues can be most welcome. Ask them to conduct an objective and searching examination of your model, checking it for both logic and applicability to the business. Most people find it easier to find fault in others' work – exploit this fact to improve **your** models and offer your services on a similar basis in return.

User Approval

Regularly present your model, or those parts of it about which you have most doubt, to your users. Do so in a manner that encourages them to work with you to find and resolve errors and omissions. Seek out exceptions and limits. When armed with a 100% understanding, the designers can work on producing the optimum database design for perhaps the 82% that needs computerized support (the normal 80:20 rule with that extra 2%, which should massively reduce the maintenance workload).

Rules

In the conventions described earlier, rules and guidelines were given. These have been summarized below for your convenience.

Quality of Entities

The basic quality assurance is simply:

*"Are they **really** entities?"*

that is, things of **real** significance about which information needs to be known or held.

Entity Checklist

- singular meaningful name?
- mutual exclusivity
- at least two attributes?
- probably no more than eight attributes?
- synonyms/homonyms
- full definition?
- volumetric information?
- a unique identifier?
- at least one relationship?
- at least one business function to create, retrieve, update, delete, archive and use the entity?
- distributed requirements?
- changes over time?
- does it conform to the principles of data normalization?
- does the entity already exist in other application systems, perhaps under a different name?
- is it too generic?
- is it sufficiently generic?

Sub-type Checklist

- are they mutually exclusive?
- does it have any attributes and/or relationships?
- do they all have their own unique identifier or share that of their super-type?
- is this the full set of possible sub-types?
- should **type** be modelled using one of the alternative methods shown in Chapter 7?
- is it really just an example of an entity?
- do you know the attributes and/or relationships and conditions that differentiate one sub-type from another?

Quality of Attributes

*"Are they **really** attributes?"*

That is, do they describe, in some way, the particular entity in question?

Attribute Checklist

– singular meaningful name?
– name should not include the entity name?
– only one value per attribute?
– no repeating values (or groups)?
– definition for format, length, allowed values, derivation, and so on?
– is it really a missing entity, perhaps required by another existing or subsequent application system?
– is it really a missing relationship?
– is it replicated from elsewhere, as a 'design feature', which perhaps needs removing at the business level?
– is it important to know different values over time?
– does its value depend only on the entity in question?
– if mandatory, would you always know its value?
– do we need a domain for this attribute and others of its kind?
– is the value of this attribute dependent on only part of the unique identifier?
– is the value of this attribute dependent on some attributes that are not part of the unique identifier?

Quality of Relationships

*"Are they **really** significant associations between entities?"*

Relationship Checklist

– each end named, and capable of being read accurately and sensibly via the syntax?
– does it only have two ends?
– test each end using the inverted syntax – is it still correct? (see Chapter 3)
– is the relationship transferable?
– each end has a degree and optionality?
– valid construct?
  $\gg\!\!-\!\!-\!\!\ll$, for example, is invalid (see Appendix B)
– rare construct? By the end of detailed analysis there should be very few one to one or many to many relationships.
– is the relationship redundant?
– does it cater for time?
– if mandatory would you always be able to connect to an entity at the other end?

Exclusive Relationship
Checklist

– all relationship ends of the same optionality?
– all relationship ends from the same entity?
– normally arcs cross the many end - is this the case?
– a relationship can only be in one arc
– are all or no relationship ends part of unique identifiers?

Completeness Check

Check through all existing system documentation, clerical forms, reports, and so on. Can you find any data item that is neither an attribute nor derivable from attributes on this model **and** is required? If so, add the missing attributes.

Print out the reports from your CASE software and check with your users for completeness.

Prepare 'business views' for all of your intersection entities. Do they correlate with existing file layouts? (See Appendix G.)

Check each elementary business function. Does it reference known entities explicitly or implicitly by recorded synonyms? Does any of its processing logic reference data not represented by attributes? Are missing relationships implied?

Check different business units for concepts that may only apply in certain locations. Have you volumetric information by business unit, if necessary?

Summary

This task need not take many days, but its value can be far-reaching, by minimizing the resultant amount of change necessary and thus increasing the productivity of your development team.

11

PRESENTATION TO SENIOR MANAGEMENT

Management Direction

Entity relationship modelling, when done well, focuses on the really key information in an organization. This is the information that there is most of, such as coupons, or that is most critical, such as crew assignments or safety checks. Management **will** therefore be keenly interested in the **detail** in these areas, which affect their business at its heart. And you should therefore be encouraged to check these models in detail with the key executives who **really** understand what the business needs to be doing. They must be given the opportunity to direct you in the appropriate way forward for the business.

But don't just show them the whole diagram.

Build it up carefully whilst illustrating **how** they perceive the business should be run. Use topical examples they recognize, and run through recent issues they have been involved with to demonstrate how your new model could help cater for their problems. As a guide, it might take thirty or forty subset diagrams to explore the detail of Altantis Airline Flights.

Once confirmed, an entity relationship model serves several purposes. In the first instance it forms an architectural framework for developing new or revised systems. It also provides a 'first-cut' database design. But successful companies have also continued to use them at a senior management level, to act as a catalyst to discussions on new ideas.

Summary Diagrams

When presenting the conclusion of a strategic enterprise model, or even a requirement definition, it is useful to have simplified diagrams to illustrate direction, as opposed to acting as definitive models. Two techniques have been found to be most useful: these are the concepts of Data Subject Areas and Overview Diagrams.

Data Subject Areas

The diagram below is **not** an entity relationship model. It is a picture where the boxes represent conceptually-useful groupings of entities, attributes and relationships. These groups are defined subjectively as being related to the same **subject**, where the subject often relates to a major functional area of the business.

Figure 11-1
A Data Subject Area Diagram

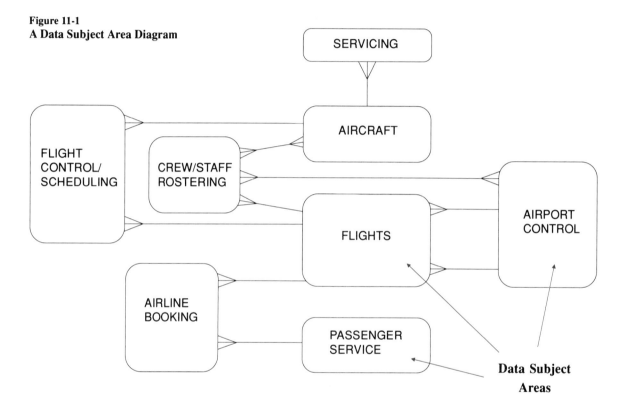

On this picture the lines simply represent some form of link or interface between different data subject areas. (They are **not** relationships, but are drawn in a similar way to avoid introducing new symbols.) The data subject area for AIRLINE BOOKING may in reality cover TICKETs, SEATs, SEAT CLASS, SEAT BOOKINGs, BOARDING PASSes and any other entities or relationships necessary to encompass that subject.

Management like these diagrams as they look simple (*"Our business is really very straightforward you know"*) and use words that correspond approximately to those they already talk about.

To the analysts they also provide yet another opportunity for testing and completeness.

"Do we actually have enough information to cover PASSENGER SERVICE yet?"

If not, we may well start a new line of questioning based on decomposing this subject area into more detail.

"Would you take me through the life-cycle of passenger service, as I believe we may have missed a few vital areas?"

Overview Diagram

In this case, the picture we use is a simplified entity relationship model. It is derived by asking the question:

*"What are the **really** significant entities and what could we sensibly leave out without removing the essence of the model?"*

Mechanistically this means hiding some sub-types, ignoring some entities and relationships, removing all but one or two attributes and removing all unique identifiers. It is often useful to merge entities that are parallel (i.e. they are related to the same entities) on the diagram and give both names of the newly-created box. Similarly relationships can be merged and the relationship end names simplified; it can be sensible to name most of them only at the **many** end to remove unnecessary clutter.

In the process of simplification, try to keep the shape of the diagram much the same as the original on which it is based; this helps understanding.

Hiding Sub-types

Figures 11-2 and 11-3 illustrate how part of a diagram may be modified to hide sub-types whilst retaining the significance of the original relationships.

Figure 11-2
Model with Sub-types

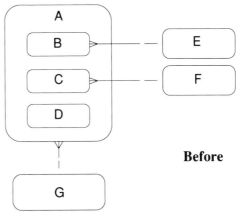

Before

Figure 11-3
Simplified Model with
Sub-types Hidden

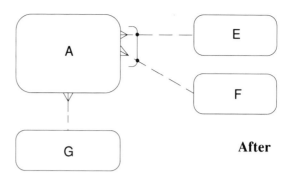

After

On the example shown below, sub-types have been hidden for entities such as AIRCRAFT and FLIGHT. Most of the entities concerning standard crew membership have been removed as these are covered adequately at this level by the single entity CREW ASSIGNMENT. SEAT BOOKING and BOARDING PASS have been merged, so an exclusive arc has been added across the relationships for SEAT and AIRCRAFT to maintain understanding.

Figure 11-4
An Overview Diagram

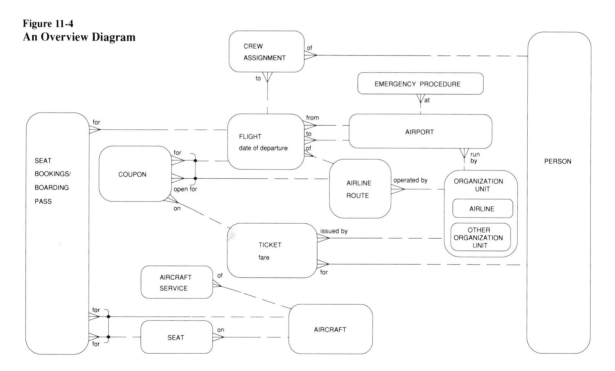

Summary

It is important to involve the appropriate senior management with the detail of their business, but they also like to see that their business is straightforward and easy to control when well understood.

Appendix

A   DATA NORMALIZATION

The Purpose

Normalization of data is a procedure to ensure that a data model conforms to some useful standards. For data and entity relationship models, these standards have been defined to minimize duplication of data, to provide the flexibility necessary to support different functional requirements, and to enable the model to be mapped onto a wide variety of alternative database designs.

Entity Modelling

Entity relationship modelling tends to produce entities that are naturally normalized. This is because we go through a simple process as follows:

- Discern the things of significance about which information needs to be known or held. These entities must be mutually exclusive, and are represented on a diagram by means of a box with the entity name in singular and in upper case.

- Add to these the business relationships, which are named significant associations between entities. These relationships are shown as a line between two boxes; each end has degree (a triangle or 'crowsfoot' means many, no triangle means one) and optionality (a dotted line means optional, a solid line means mandatory).

- For each entity we list the types of information that might be held or known. These attributes are shown within the entity as names in lower case.

- Finally, we ascertain how each occurrence of an entity may be uniquely identified. This will be by some combination of attributes and/or relationships. When an attribute is part of the unique identifier it is shown by a # mark. When a relationship end is part of the unique identifier it is shown by a bar across the relationship line.

Following the above process rigorously will automatically give a normalized model, but it does rely upon the analyst thoroughly understanding what an attribute, relationship and entity really are. The three formal rules of Third Normal Form (TNF) are given below and their application is illustrated on the diagrams.

Normalization

To check that an entity relationship model that has all its entities uniquely identified has been fully normalized and thus conforms to Third Normal Form, the following simple tests can be applied.

Precursor

Ensure that all entities are uniquely identifiable by a combination of attributes and/or relationships.

First Normal Form

Remove repeated attributes or groups of attributes.

If there is more than one value at a time for an attribute or more than one attribute with the same name, we define a new entity, which is described by that attribute. The unique identifier of this new entity comprises one of the attributes that migrated to it and the relationship (many to one) to the original entity.

For example, remove the crew-1, crew-2, crew-3 groups of attributes. A new entity, CREW MEMBER, is created, defined by name and role attributes and with a many to one relationship to the original FLIGHT entity. (See 1NF on the diagrams.)

First normal form is thus a mechanism for identifying missing entities and relationships.

Second Normal Form

Remove attributes dependent on only part of the unique identifier.

If an entity has a unique identifier composed of more than one attribute and/or relationship, and if another attribute depends on only **part** of that composite identifier, then the attribute and the part of the identifier on which it is dependent should form the basis of a new entity. The new entity is identified by the migrated part of the unique identifier of the original entity, and has a one to many relationship to the original entity.

For example, the attribute flight number does not have a value that is dependent upon the flight's date and time. We will have, instead, a standard AIRLINE ROUTE with a fixed flight number, which may be scheduled as one or more FLIGHTS over a period of time. (See 2NF on the diagrams.)

Second normal form is also a mechanism for identifying missing entities and relationships.

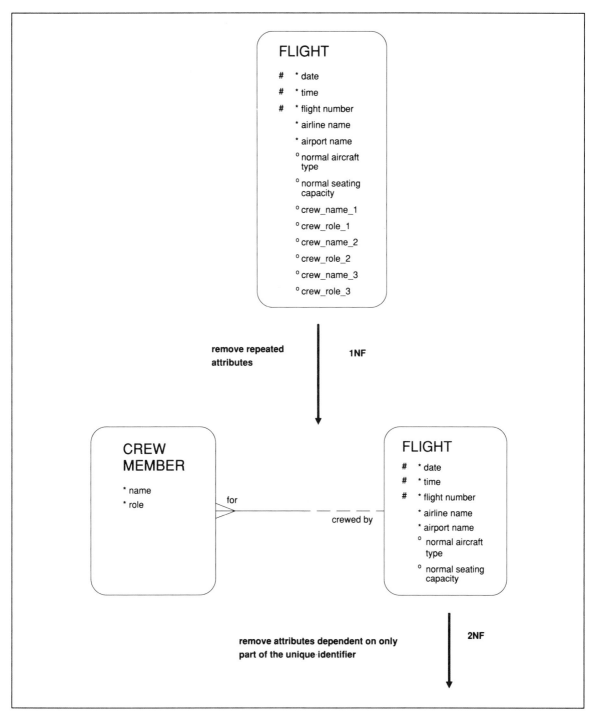

Third Normal Form	*Remove attributes dependent on attributes that are not part of the unique identifier.*

If an attribute of an entity is dependent on another attribute, which is not part of the unique identifier, then these attributes should form the basis of a new entity, which has a one to many relationship to the original entity. The unique identifier for the new entity is that attribute upon which the other attribute is dependent.

For example, airline name, aircraft type and normal seating capacity of an aircraft do not have values that are dependent upon the flight number of an AIRLINE ROUTE. Hopefully it is the president of the airline who decides its name, not someone who allocates routes and schedules flights! (See 3NF on the diagrams.)

Third normal form is our final mechanism for identifying missing entities and relationships.

Intuitive Normalization

If you examine the resultant model carefully you will realize that a good analyst would have already worked out that there are separate things of significance about which information needs to be held (entities) for each of AIRPORT, AIRLINE, PERSON, etc. The analyst would also have realized that an airline name could **only** be an attribute of an airline. If the airline name appears elsewhere on paper, it will often be because it is a convenient way of implementing a significant business relationship from something to the airline; for example, the airline name might be printed on the schedule of routes.

If the crew 'role' is really 'role type' with a small set of predefined values (e.g. captain) then this would break third normal form and yet another entity (called say CREW MEMBER TYPE) would need to be created.

Notice also that in the final model we have brought out a new entity called PERSON and defined a role of a person as that of CREW ASSIGNMENT to a FLIGHT. This will prove useful later as a point of flexibility, when we add a PASSENGER role between PERSON and FLIGHT, which allows crew to be passengers on other flights. The model is still inaccurate as we cannot uniquely identify PERSON, and there are obviously many missing attributes, entities and relationships - the useful thing is that this process has considerably helped move our understanding forward.

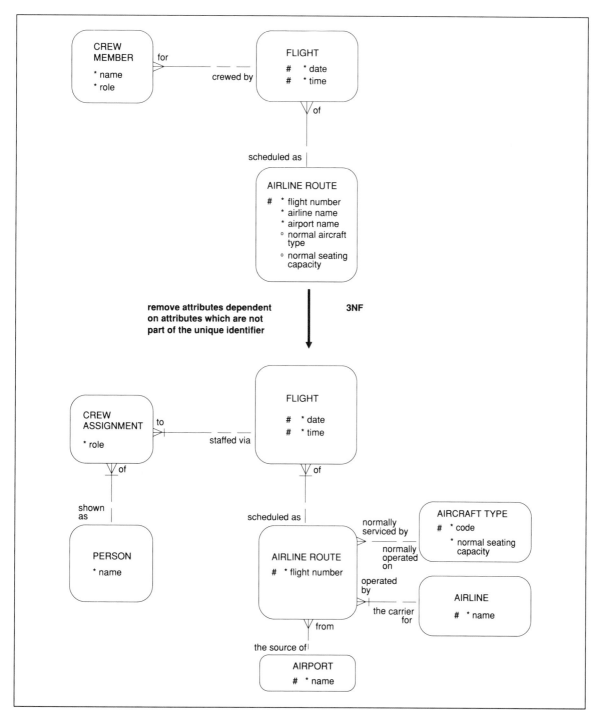

Terminology

It is also interesting to note that in the final mode, flight number should really be renamed route number. This terminology problem is typical of most businesses – in the airline industry the word flight will be used to mean both ROUTE and FLIGHT, often in the same sentence. That's life!

Mathematical Definitions

For those of you who might find it interesting, we have provided the following precise definitions, taken from the book by C. J. Date *An Introduction to Database Systems Volume 1* 4th edition, © 1986, Addison-Wesley Publishing Co., Inc., Reading, Massachusetts (reprinted with permission of the publisher), and have covered the concepts up to fifth normal form.

Terminology

The terminology used here is specifically for pure relational theory, as opposed to the entity relationship business modelling we have been addressing, but the principles still apply.

General

"A relation R is in third normal form (3NF) if and only if, for all time, each tuple of R consists of a primary key value that identifies some entity, together with a set of zero or more mutually independent attribute values that describe that entity in some way."

1NF

"A relation R is in first normal form (1NF) if and only if all underlying domains contain atomic values only."

2NF

"A relation R is in second normal form (2NF) if and only if it is in 1NF and every nonkey attribute is fully dependent on the primary key."

3NF

"A relation R is in third normal form (3NF) if and only if it is in 2NF and every nonkey attribute is nontransitively dependent on the primary key."

Boyce/Codd

"A relation R is in Boyce/Codd normal form (BCNF) if and only if every determinant is a candidate key."

4NF

"A relation R is in fourth normal form (4NF) if and only if, wherever there exists an MVD in R, say $A \rightarrow \rightarrow B$, then all attributes of R are also functionally dependent on A. In other words, the only dependencies (FDs or MVDs) in R are of the form $K \rightarrow X$ (i.e., a functional dependency from a candidate key K to some other attribute X). Equivalently: R is in 4NF if it is in BCNF and all MVDs in R are in fact FDs."

FD = Functional Dependency, MVD = Multivalued Dependency

5NF

"A relation R is in fifth normal form (5NF)—also called projection-join normal form (PJ/NF)—if and only if every join dependency in R is a consequence of the candidate keys of R."

All of these definitions assume each tuple can be uniquely identified by the values of a set of attributes that constitute the primary key.

Beyond 3NF with Entity Relationship Modelling

The same principles apply to business level models and the following simple questions will help you conform to these rigorous principles in a more straightforward manner.

Look around the business and ask yourself:

"Have I really identified every separate thing of significance?"

"Is each relationship really significant, or is it just required for the duration of a function?"

"Should an attribute really be a relationship to something else?"

"Is an attribute something of significance in its own right, possibly from someone else's perspective - in which case it may be better modelled as an entity."

"Are entities with similar sets of attributes and/or relationships in fact different perceptions or states of the same thing?"

Data Denormalization

Data denormalization is the reverse procedure, carried out purely for reasons of improving performance of production systems, particularly when these are computerized. Denormalization must only be performed on the design.

Never compromise the business model.

Classical examples of denormalization include the controlled replication of data. For example, it may be more efficient for a high-throughput airline booking system to replicate the data item for normal seating capacity onto the flight details. The disadvantage is, however, that flight details will now use more storage capacity, and, should the normal seating capacity change, then the new value will have to be replicated onto every set of flight details for that aircraft type.

A second example of denormalization would be to hold a repeating group of data on the flight details, one for each seat, indicating its seat number and availability. This form of denormalization should only be used when there are only one or two business functions that use the data. In this case, the functions would probably be to assign/reassign seats and enquire on current assignments.

Denormalization on manual procedure forms is, by necessity, very common, as is evidenced by the fact that most paper forms hold vast amounts of reference data. We all know the problems this can cause when that data is changed and the entire set of forms has to be reissued.

Appendix

B

VALID RELATIONSHIPS

The following information about the normal usage of relationship degree and optionality may be found useful.

Many to One

Figure B-1
Mandatory to Optional

This is by far the most common form of relationship. It implies that each and every instance of an A can only ever exist within the (named) context of one (and only one) B. On the other hand, Bs may exist with or without associations to As.

Figure B-2
Optional to Optional

Used occasionally. Both A and B can exist without the relationship between them.

Figure B-3
Mandatory to Mandatory

This is a very powerful construct, which implies that an instance of B cannot be created without simultaneously creating at least one associated A. On our example, a TICKET is not significant unless it is made up of at least one COUPON; until then it is just a piece of paper.

Figure B-4
Optional to Mandatory

This rare construct is once more useful when it occurs. This often occurs when B is some invented concept that always consists of a precise set of As. The As can already exist in their own right. (On closer examination, these relationships often become many to many – use inverted syntax to check them accurately.)

One to One

Figure B-5
Mandatory to Optional

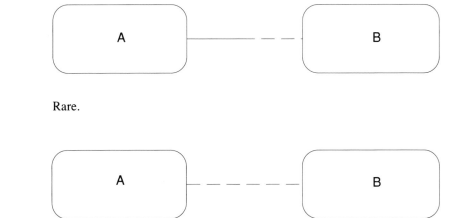

Rare.

Figure B-6
Optional to Optional

Rare.

Figure B-7
Mandatory to Mandatory

Very rare. (Nearly always wrong!)

With nearly every one to one relationship closer examination will normally show that A and B are really different views or subsets of the same thing, perhaps with different names and some different relationships or attributes. Some analysts do use one to one relationships to put overlapping or orthogonal sub-types on to a model. (See Chapter 7.)

Many to Many

Figure B-8
Optional to Optional

This construct is very common early on in an analysis and signifies a relationship that is either not fully understood and needs further resolution, or is just a simple collective association – a two-way list.

Figure B-9
Mandatory to Optional

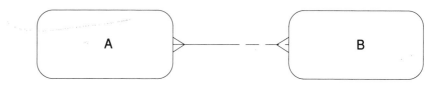

Rare. These relationships should always be resolved into further detail.

Figure B-10
Mandatory to Mandatory

Impossible. This relationship implies that no instance of an A can exist without a B and vice versa. In practice, every such construct has always been found to be inaccurate.

Recursive Relationships - Many to One

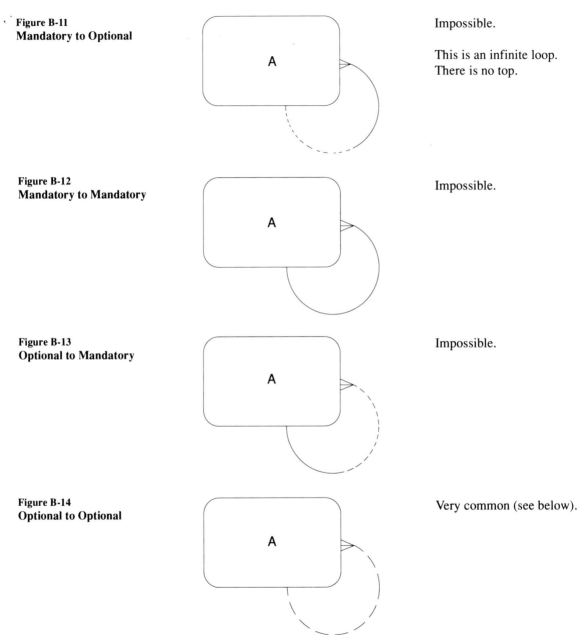

Figure B-11
Mandatory to Optional

Impossible.

This is an infinite loop.
There is no top.

Figure B-12
Mandatory to Mandatory

Impossible.

Figure B-13
Optional to Mandatory

Impossible.

Figure B-14
Optional to Optional

Very common (see below).

Very common (often called an "optional pig's ear!"). This shows a simple, any-level hierarchy and is commonly used for such things as organization hierarchies, classification for products, marketing, and so on.

One to One

Figure B-15
Mandatory to Optional

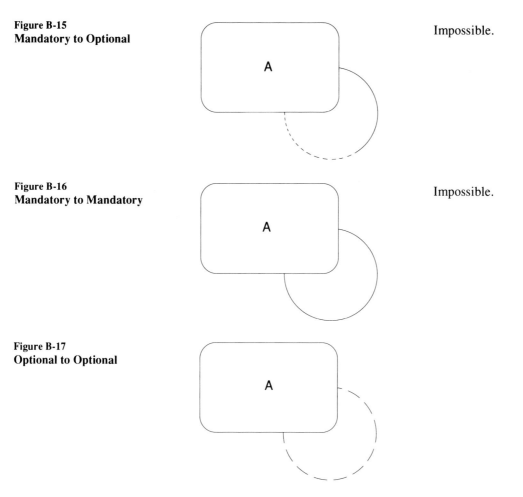

Impossible.

Figure B-16
Mandatory to Mandatory

Impossible.

Figure B-17
Optional to Optional

Rare but very useful. This could be used for relationships that show an alternative.

Many to Many

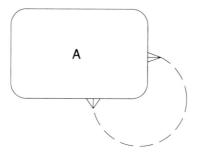

Common early on. These often imply a 'Bill of Materials' structure, showing the make-up and break-down of components.

For example:

> *Each COMPONENT may be made up of one or more (other) COMPONENTs and each COMPONENT may be used in one or more (other) COMPONENTs.*

Figure B-19
Mandatory to Optional

Impossible.

Figure B-20
Mandatory to Mandatory

Impossible.

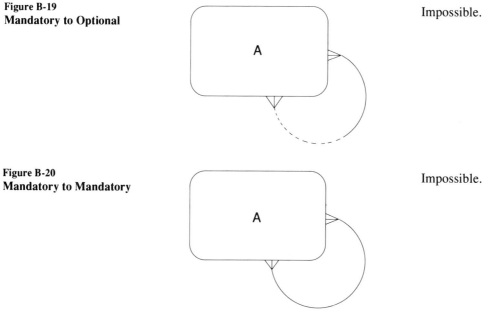

Appendix

C

DETAILED DEFINITIONS OF ENTITY, RELATIONSHIP, DOMAIN AND ATTRIBUTE

This appendix covers the detailed definitions that may be used for entity, relationship, domain and attribute. Standard paper forms are shown, but it is preferable to use a CASE system to record this information.

The forms included are:

C6	Entity Definition	(includes outline attributes, relationships, unique identifiers and basic volumes)
C7	Entity Volumes	(general volumes)
C8	Entity Volumes	(distributed requirements)
C3	Domain Definition	
C9	Full Attribute Definition.	

These forms are taken from the book *CASE*Method Tasks and Deliverables*, Appendix C. This contains a range of blank forms, which may be copied, for use with CASE*Method.

ORACLE ® ———— ENTITY DEFINITION ————

THE RELATIONAL DATABASE
MANAGEMENT SYSTEM

Reference ....*52*..........

Name (plural) *COUPON(s)* ....   Sub-type of ....

Synonyms ....   Initial Vol ....

....   Average Vol .... Likely Maximum ....

....   Growth Rate .... % per year

Description: Has significance as *a part of a ticket which may be exchanged for flight on an aircraft, often by the procedure of issuing a boarding pass.*

Attributes

Name	Optional	Domain	Format	Max. Length	Notes	See full definition	Unique Identifier
class	N	class					
status						✓	
confirmed indicator	N		char	1	Boolean		
comment	Y		char	40			

Relationships: Each occurrence of this entity

must / may be	link phrase	one and only one / one or more	entity name	cascade delete	Arc	
must be	for	one and only one	ticket	✕		✓
must be	for	one and only one	flight		1	
must be	open for	one and only one	airline route		1	✓

Notes/remarks

The full attribute definition would need to be entered for allowable values for the attributes shown with a tick in the column headed 'see full definition'.

Please turn over for detailed figures

Form
C6

Team
User

Project
Activity

Analyst
Checked by

Date
Date

Sheet ...*1*... of ...*3*...

ORACLE ® ———————— ENTITY VOLUMES —

THE RELATIONAL DATABASE
MANAGEMENT SYSTEM

(General Volumes)

Reference .52.............

Entity Name . . *COUPON* . . . .

(See distributed requirement)

Detailed Volumes (for some entities)

	Volume or % growth	Notes
Current volumes		
Projected: Period 1		
Period 2		
Period 3		
Period 4		
Period 5		

Retention

	Number	Period	Reason
Archive after			
Destroy after			

n.b. Ensure functions are included for archive and destroy,
with appropriate conditions.

Business Integrity Rules (General)

Condition	Rule
On coupon creation or allocation to a flight.	*Coupons can only be allocated for flights that have a date of departure yesterday, today and in the future. Yesterday is permitted to cater for delayed flights.*

Form
C7

Team
User

Project
Activity

Analyst
Checked by

Date
Date

Sheet .2. of .3.

ORACLE ®———————— ENTITY VOLUMES ———

THE RELATIONAL DATABASE
MANAGEMENT SYSTEM

(Distributed Requirement)

Entity Name . . . . *COUPON* . . . .

BUSINESS UNIT	From Current	New
Reference . . *BU-1*	Initial Vol	. . . .
Name . . . . *Atlantia*	Average Vol . . . . Likely Maximum . . . .
	Growth Rate . . . . % per year

Detailed Volumes (for some entities)

		Volume or % growth		Notes
Current volumes		250,000	///////	
Projected: Period 1	1989	10	%	
Period 2	1990	30	%	*Scheduled acquisition of new*
Period 3	1991	20	%	*airline routes.*
Period 4				
Period 5				

Retention

	Number	Period	Reason
Archive after	3	*months*	
Destroy after	9	*months*	

n.b. Ensure functions are included for archive and destroy,
with appropriate conditions.

Special business unit specific Integrity Rules

Condition	Rule

Entity Definition

To fully define an entity the following properties are required, as shown by the standard forms C6 and C7, or as prompted for by a CASE product. Where information is used across a geographically-dispersed organization it is important to record distributed requirements for entities using form C8 in conjunction with form C6.

The entity definition form allows the recording of attribute name, optionality, domain, format, notes and whether the attribute is part of a unique identifier. This is sufficient for most attributes. When there is a further attribute definition required, form C9 is used (which also defines these attribute properties in detail).

Entity Properties

	Strategy	Analysis	Rules
Name	M	M	Unique within context. Singular. Agreed by users. Unambiguous.
Plural	M	M	Unique within context. Used as agreed format for sentences needing plural.
Synonym(s)	O	O	Alternative names for the same thing.
Example(s)	O	O	May be recorded under notes to ensure full understanding.
Description	O	M	A terse, precise, user-agreed definition of the entity, ideally starting with the phrase "Entity-name has significance as ..."
Notes/remarks	O	O	To contain useful information about the entity, for use by other analysts or designers.
Reference	O	O	A unique reference, if required by the installation.
Sub-type of	M	M	Only one allowed, and must be included if known.

Legend   M   =   mandatory
                 O   =   optional

Association of Entity with Other Elements

	Strategy	Analysis	Rules
Attribute	O	M	During strategy one or two are useful. At least two must exist per entity by the end of analysis.
Function	O	M	During strategy a cross-check is useful. At the end of analysis there should be at least one function per entity for create, update, delete and other usage. This is normally shown on a function definition form.
Relationship	M	M	Details of relationships to all other entities. Each entity must be related to at least one other entity. (See relationship details below.)
Business unit (distributed requirement)	O	O	For distributed organizations the volume of each entity by business unit/department may be essential. See standard form C8.

Using a dictionary (encyclopedia or repository) this information may be cross-checked quickly, and easily produced as a report for user agreement.

Integrity Rules

Integrity Rules	O	O	In some cases these are vital, reflecting inherent business rules as opposed to transient policy, and may be recorded on form C7 or C8 as appropriate.
Legend M = mandatory O = optional			

Volumetrics

	Strategy	Analysis	Rules
Volumes	O	M	This may be as simple as a single value (e.g. 200 aircraft), in which case enter values for initial, average, maximum volume and growth rate on form C6. If it needs to reflect ranges, growth rates by period, and distribution across the organization then use form C7. Volumes of sub-types should approximately coincide with those for their super-types.
Retention	O	O	Unless information is eventually archived or destroyed systems grind to a halt. This should be filled in for all high volume entities on form C7 or C8.
Legend M = mandatory O = optional			

Relationship Definition

To fully define a relationship the following properties are required for each end. See form C6.

Relationship Properties

	Strategy	Analysis	Rules
Degree	M	M	Qualified degrees may be appropriate.
End name	M	M	This link phrase should be precedable by the phrase **must/may be**
Optionality	M	M	Either optional or mandatory.
Note/remark	O	O	For special cases.
Minimum degree	O	O	Enter details in the Notes as required.
Average degree	O	O	Enter details in the Notes.
Maximum degree	O	O	Enter details in the Notes.

Cascade Delete Indicator

Cascade Delete Indicator	O	O	C = Cascade delete if parent deleted. X = Inhibit parent deletion if child still exists. N = Either child or parent may be deleted separately.
Legend M = mandatory O = optional			

Association of Relationship with Other Elements

	Strategy	Analysis	Rules
Entity	M	M	Each end must be associated with an entity.
Function	O	O	Occasionally a function will need to refer explicitly to the connection or disconnection of a relationship.
Arc	O	O	Each relationship end may be in one and only one arc, indicated by showing all the relationship ends within an arc with the same name/number in the column labelled 'arc'.

Unique Identifier

Two columns are set aside on the entity definition form to enable the recording of two alternative unique identifiers. The columns enable each unique identifier to be a combination of attributes and/or relationship ends, by ticking against the appropriate entries. By the end of analysis each entity should have a unique identifier.

	Strategy	Analysis	Rules
Unique Identifier	O	O	Each relationship end may be quoted as a component in one or more unique identifiers.
Legend M	=	mandatory	
O	=	optional	

Until one becomes a little practised, it may be time-consuming to think up useful relationship names.

Useful Pairs of Relationship Names

about	subject of
applicable to	context for*
at	location of
based on	basis for
based on	under
bought in from	supplier of
bound by	for
change authority for	on
classification for	of
covered by	for
defined by	part definition of
description of	for
for	shown on
for work under	authority for
initiated by	initiator of
nominee for	subject of
notified on	notification point for
operated by	operator for
owned by	owner of*
part of	composed of
part of	detailed by
party to	for
party to	holder of
placed on	responsible for
precluded by	precluded by
represented by	representation of
responsible for	responsibility of
responsible for	of
run by	carrier for
source of	based on

Useful Pairs of Relationship Names

trigger for	triggered by
under	context for
verified by	verifier of
within	responsible for

Note: where the above are marked with an asterisk*, one should only use these as a last resort. For example, owned by should only be used as a relationship name when the relationship means legal ownership.

Some of the above names imply the role of a person or an organization.

ORACLE ®————— DOMAIN DEFINITION —
THE RELATIONAL DATABASE (BUSINESS LEVEL)
MANAGEMENT SYSTEM

Domain Name *CLASS*   Subset of domain

Description/notes
Defines the allowable values for classifications of air travel, as applicable to COUPONs and SEATs.

Format	Max Length	Average	Unit of Measure
char	*8*	*7*	

	User	Access right (C,U,D,A,R,All)	Authority Level
Available to			
Responsibility of			

Validation rule

Normal default value	*Economy*
Value for null	

Normal Derivation

Value	High Value	Abbreviation	Meaning
Business		*B*	*Business or Clipper Class*
Economy		*E*	*Economy or Cabin Class*
First		*F*	*First Class*

Domain Definition

To fully define a domain the following properties are required, as shown on standard form C3.

	Strategy	**Analysis**	**Rules**
Name	O	O	Short names are useful to speed up cross-referencing.
Description	O	M	
Format	O	M	Character, integer, date, ...
Maximum length	O	M	
Average length	O	O	
Unit of measure	O	O	
User available to	O	O	Sometimes domains such as salary have restricted access for all attributes in the domain. This is rare.
Access right	O	O	For rights such as Create a value, Update, Delete, Archive, Retrieve/Read/ Select.
Authority level	O	O	Salary levels may be accessible to users, controlled by levels.
Responsibility of	O	O	Domains that implement corporate business rules may be the responsibility of a certain user role.
Validation rule	O	O	Often an algorithm or list of values (see below).
Normal default value	O	O	Very rare, as 'default' implies we would always be happy with the value given by default.

	Strategy	Analysis	Rules
Value for null	O	O	In some implementations null has to be reserved a specific value to mean 'there is no current value!' When such an implementation tool is anticipated it is sensible to agree with users early on which particular value would practicably be used for null. (See Glossary.)
Normal derivation	O	O	
A set of values or ranges value	O	O	An explicit value (or the low value when a range is applicable).
high value	O	O	
abbreviation	O	O	A user-agreed abbreviation.
meaning	O	O	The full meaning of the value or range.

Association with Other Elements

	Strategy	Analysis	Rules
Domain	O	O	A domain may be within another domain and inherit its constraints as well.
Attribute	O	O	At the end of analysis it is only sensible that each domain qualifies at least two attributes.
Legend M = mandatory O = optional			

ORACLE ®————— FULL ATTRIBUTE DEFINITION —

THE RELATIONAL DATABASE
MANAGEMENT SYSTEM

Name . *status* . . . . of entity . *COUPON* . . . . in domain . . . .

Description/note

Indicates the states that a coupon may be in for analysis purposes; e.g. to analyze how many coupons are created but not collected.

Mandatory/Optional

. . . . % initially   on condition . . . .

. . . . % normally   . . . .

Format	Max. Length	Average Length	Unit of Measure
char	. . . *1*	. . . .	. . . .

	User	Access right (C,U,D,A,R,All)	Authority/Level
Available to	. . . .	. . . .	
	. . . .	. . . .	
	. . . .	. . . .	
Responsibility of	. . . .	. . . .	

Validation Rule

The following table shows valid state changes:

From	To
1	*2, 3, 6, 7, 9*
2	*3, 6, 9*

Default value . . . .   (only if mandatory)

Value for null . . . .   (only if optional)

Derivation *When a coupon is created, the status is set to 1.*

Value	High Value	Abbreviation	Meaning
1			*Created*
2			*Collected or issued*
3			*Used normally*
6			*Transferred or replaced*
7			*Cashed in for money*
9			*Void*

Attribute Definition

To fully define an attribute the following properties are required, as shown on standard form C9.

	Strategy	Analysis	Rules
Name	O	O	Not essential, but very useful. Short names are useful to speed up cross-referencing.
Description	O	M	
Mandatory/ optional	O	M	
% initially	O	O	Only if optional. Useful for design of data take-on.
% normally	O	O	Only if optional. Useful for design and sizing of storage mechanisms.
On condition	O	O	Only for optional to define the condition when a value must exist.
Format	O	M	Character, integer, date, ...
Maximum length	O	M	
Average length	O	O	
Unit of measure	O	O	
User available to	O	O	Sometimes domains such as salary have restricted access for all attributes in the domain. This is rare.
Access right	O	O	For rights such as Create a value, Update, Delete, Archive, Retrieve/Read/ Select.
Authority/ Level	O	O	Salary levels may be accessible to users, controlled by levels.

	Strategy	Analysis	Rules
Responsibility of	O	O	Domains that implement corporate business rules may be the responsibility of a certain user role.
Validation rule	O	O	Often an algorithm or list of values (see below).
Default rule	O	O	Very rare, as 'default' implies we would always be happy with the value given by default. Only required if the attribute is mandatory.
Value for null	O	O	In some implementations null has to be reserved a specific value to mean 'there is no current value!' When such an implementation tool is anticipated it is sensible to agree with users early on which particular value would practicably be used for null. Only required if the attribute is optional. (See Glossary.)
Derivation	O	O	A calculation, count or similar algorithm (rare).
A set of values or ranges: value	O	O	An explicit value (or the low value when a range is applicable).
high value	O	O	
abbreviation	O	O	A user-agreed abbreviation.
meaning	O	O	The full meaning of the value or range.
Legend M = mandatory O = optional			

Association with Other Elements

	Strategy	Analysis	Rules
Entity	M	M	Attributes can only exist in the context of an entity.
Domain	O	O	An attribute may be constrained by the definition of a domain, but only if the domain covers at least one other attribute.
Function	O	M	Each attribute must be used by functions, implicitly via an entity or explicitly, to set value, change value or optionally nullify value, either explicitly.
Legend M = mandatory O = optional			

D   Use of CASE Tools

Computer-Aided Systems (or Software) Engineering (CASE) tools are available from many different vendors. Most offer some form of entity relationship or data modelling capability. The following overview diagrams are designed to give you some insight into what to look for from these products during each of the stages of the Business System Life Cycle. The Strategy and Analysis stages are illustrated in more detail to show in which sequence you might wish to use the facilities within the CASE tools to support entity relationship modelling.

The diagrams, however, in no way indicate the tasks that need to be performed within these stages: these are defined in another book entitled *CASE*Method – Tasks and Deliverables*, which was written by the author of this book in collaboration with several other world-class analysts, designers and project leaders.

CASE SUPPORT
for the
BUSINESS SYSTEM LIFE CYCLE

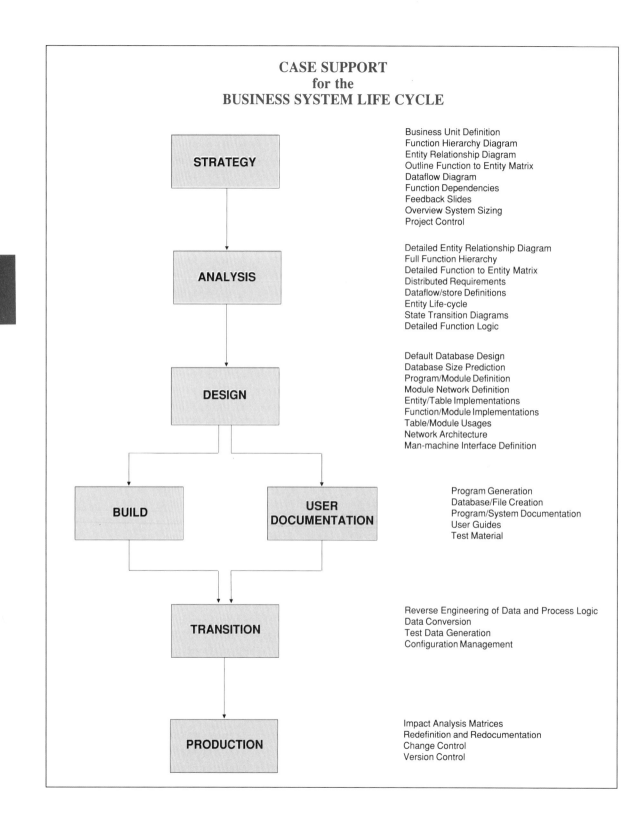

STRATEGY

Business Unit Definition
Function Hierarchy Diagram
Entity Relationship Diagram
Outline Function to Entity Matrix
Dataflow Diagram
Function Dependencies
Feedback Slides
Overview System Sizing
Project Control

ANALYSIS

Detailed Entity Relationship Diagram
Full Function Hierarchy
Detailed Function to Entity Matrix
Distributed Requirements
Dataflow/store Definitions
Entity Life-cycle
State Transition Diagrams
Detailed Function Logic

DESIGN

Default Database Design
Database Size Prediction
Program/Module Definition
Module Network Definition
Entity/Table Implementations
Function/Module Implementations
Table/Module Usages
Network Architecture
Man-machine Interface Definition

BUILD

USER DOCUMENTATION

Program Generation
Database/File Creation
Program/System Documentation
User Guides
Test Material

TRANSITION

Reverse Engineering of Data and Process Logic
Data Conversion
Test Data Generation
Configuration Management

PRODUCTION

Impact Analysis Matrices
Redefinition and Redocumentation
Change Control
Version Control

STRATEGY STAGE

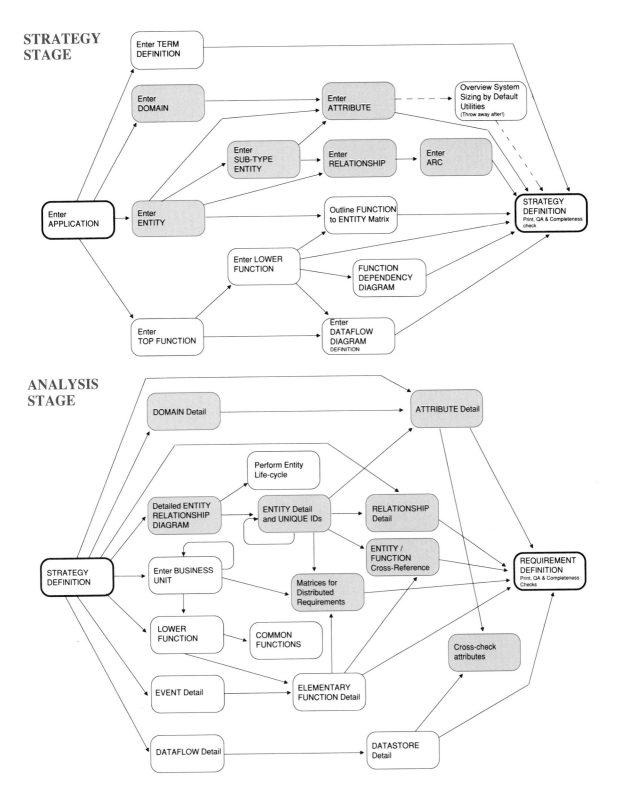

Enter TERM DEFINITION

Enter DOMAIN

Enter ATTRIBUTE

Overview System Sizing by Default Utilities (Throw away after!)

Enter SUB-TYPE ENTITY

Enter RELATIONSHIP

Enter ARC

Enter APPLICATION

Enter ENTITY

Outline FUNCTION to ENTITY Matrix

STRATEGY DEFINITION
Print, QA & Completeness check

Enter LOWER FUNCTION

FUNCTION DEPENDENCY DIAGRAM

Enter TOP FUNCTION

Enter DATAFLOW DIAGRAM DEFINITION

ANALYSIS STAGE

DOMAIN Detail

ATTRIBUTE Detail

Perform Entity Life-cycle

Detailed ENTITY RELATIONSHIP DIAGRAM

ENTITY Detail and UNIQUE IDs

RELATIONSHIP Detail

STRATEGY DEFINITION

Enter BUSINESS UNIT

ENTITY / FUNCTION Cross-Reference

Matrices for Distributed Requirements

REQUIREMENT DEFINITION
Print, QA & Completeness Checks

LOWER FUNCTION

COMMON FUNCTIONS

EVENT Detail

ELEMENTARY FUNCTION Detail

Cross-check attributes

DATAFLOW Detail

DATASTORE Detail

Use of CASE Tools   D-3

Summary

Multi-user, team-oriented CASE tools with modern interactive diagrammers and appropriate utilities and reporting capability can help you improve the quality of your models and the productivity of your key strategists and analysts.

Access control, version control and project management capability are then essential for your data administrator and project leaders to help them control this vital data about your business.

Appendix

E

DATA ADMINISTRATION

**Data Administration
The Role**

The definition of data administration encompasses the recording, quality checking and custodianship of all the information relating to the business system that is being analyzed and subsequently engineered.

This information is now recognized by many organizations as being vital to the success of their data processing and management information. As a consequence, someone senior is usually appointed in this role. Ideally the person not only understands the concepts in this book (and otherwise defined in the appendices) but also has a clear and accurate understanding of the business to which they relate and the objects it is trying to achieve.

In simple terms the role includes ensuring that, for example, entity definitions are complete, accurate and agreed. Of more importance is recognizing the opportunity for generic modelling, resolving conflicting requirements, ensuring that there is at least **one** practicable way of implementing any concept and administering access to these definitions.

Control

The job is made more difficult when large-scale situations are concerned. In nearly all cases, it is vital to have a shared dictionary or repository built on top of a good database to maintain all the data and cross-references. Reports from such CASE tools can then help on quality, completeness and impact analysis work.

In large businesses one may start off with an enterprise-wide set of models, which are then subsetted for different application systems. These systems invariably overlap, have different teams working on them and repeatedly go through incremental rolling change as they move from one version to another. Simultaneously one might have a system with a version in production, another under development and a third version being conceived – with any or all of these overlapping with other systems.

A data administrator therefore needs some form of sophisticated CASE tool to help control:

- access to the definitions
- privileges for change
- definition of systems
- version and change control.

Typically a data administrator would work closely with end users, leading analysts on different projects and the database designers.

A Key Role

Data Administration is a key role. It must not be neglected if you intend to produce high-quality, end-user-oriented, flexible systems.

Appendix

F

RELATIONAL DATABASE DESIGN

This book is not intended to be a definitive guide to database design, but it was felt that the basic technique of logical relational database design from an entity relationship model should be illustrated. Some basic knowledge of Structured Query Language (SQL) as defined by the American National Standards Institute (ANSI) is assumed.

Simple Database Design

Step 1

Each simple entity is translated to a table. A simple entity is one which is not a sub-type or has sub-types of its own. A useful standard is to use the plural form of the entity for the table name.

Step 2

Each attribute is translated into a candidate column of the same name, at which time a more precise **format** may be chosen.

> Optional attributes become **null** columns.
> Mandatory attributes becomes **not-null** columns.

Step 3

The components of the unique identifier of the entity become the primary key of the table. Remember that there may be more than one unique identifier for an entity – the most-used one is chosen.

Remember also that an entity may be uniquely identified by a combination of attributes and/or relationships. When relationships are used, follow along the relationship and bring down as columns a copy of the unique identification components of the entity at the far end of the relationship as part of the primary key. (This may be recursive until attributes are eventually found.)

During this process, relationship end names and/or entity names are used with the attribute names to suggest unique column names for use as part of foreign keys.

Step 4

Many to one (and one to one) relationships become foreign keys. That is, bring down a copy of the unique identifier of each referenced entity from the **one** end and use as candidate columns.

Optional relationships create **null** columns.
Mandatory relationships create **not-null** columns.

Figure F-1
Example

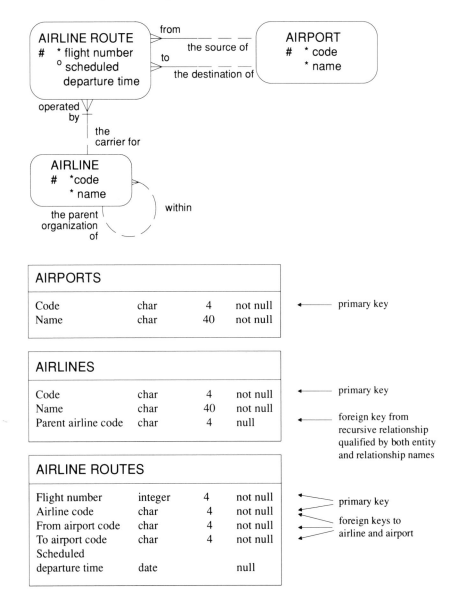

Steps 1 to 4 represent by far the majority of normal logical design situations. Before we have a look at the more complex cases where exclusivity and sub-types are used, let us have a brief look at indexes.

Step 5
Index Design

Create candidate indexes for each of the:

– primary key (unique index)
– foreign keys and
– those suggested by any Function:Attribute matrix.

Remember the primary key and foreign keys may each be comprised of more than one column.

Where a column is the first quoted column in a multi-column index, it need not normally be indexed in its own right for other purposes.

A thorough, detailed analysis may result in function definitions that quote the usage of attributes for selection conditions. In these cases a matrix of function to attributes may have been created, where the most-used attributes, when mapped down to columns of tables, are used as candidate indexes.

Subsequent performance monitoring of your RDBMS will help you establish which indexes are used and in what circumstances.

Example

Indexes on the above three tables would be as follows:

AIRPORTS code	(Unique index)
AIRLINES code	(Unique index)
AIRLINES Parent airline code	(Non-unique index)
AIRLINE ROUTES Flight number and Airline code	(Multi-column unique index)
AIRLINE ROUTES From airport code	(Non-unique index)
AIRLINE ROUTES To airport code	(Non-unique index)

Step 6
Design for Sub-types

An entity sub-type is simply an entity with its own attributes or relationships, but it also inherits any attributes and/or relationships from its parent entity (super-type) and so on up the hierarchy of super-types.

For those of you who have used object-oriented data structures with inheritance properties you will find the concept familiar.

There are two basic alternatives, each with its own advantages and disadvantages:

- all in one table
- table for sub-types.

All in One Table

A table is created for the outer super-type entity and optional relational **views** may be created for each of the sub-types. As before, attributes and many to one relationships cause candidate columns for data and foreign keys to be created.

A view is a means of accessing a subset of a table as if it were a second table. The view may be restricted to a subset of columns or to specific rows and may change column names. These simple views may be used for update as well as retrieval. (More complex views including data from many tables and derived data may also be created, but normally for read access only.)

The same process occurs for each sub-type and for each of their sub-types and so on. The difference is that **all** candidate columns created for sub-types are made **not null** (optional). A mandatory attribute (or relationship) for one sub-type would not be applicable for another – therefore they must all be made optional and the integrity enforced either by the application software or by a view with enforced **check option**.

At least one extra non-null column must be added to the table to indicate TYPE, and it becomes part of the primary key.

For example:

TYPE   char 4   not null   with a prescribed value for every sub-type.

A relational view may be created for each of the sub-types, to enable processing to access only the data they need, as specified at the business level by business functions defining actions on entities that are sub-types. These must include derived columns for the sub-type, all of its sub-types and its super-type(s). It is possible to add a WHERE clause to the view that checks for the validity of foreign keys and the optionality of columns in the context of the **Type** column. In some relational implementations, when inserting or updating through such a view, a **WITH CHECK OPTION** clause may be used to enforce these conditions within the database management system.

Note: it is, however, recommended that such integrity enforcement is added to the application code, to ensure that users can receive meaningful, in-context messages when the integrity constraint is infringed.

Figure F-2
Example

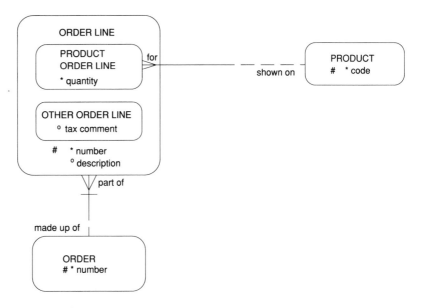

ORDER LINES			
Line_number	integer	4	not null
Order_number	integer	9	not null
Type	char	3	not null
Description	char	40	null
Tax_comment	char	40	null
Quantity	number	6,0	null
Product_code	char	6	null

- primary keys
- Type column with values 'OL', 'POL' and 'OOL' for the super-type and sub-types
- from OTHER ORDER LINE
- from PRODUCT ORDER LINE
- foreign key to PRODUCT

Note that as there are two columns called **number** both have been qualified by adjectives to keep their meaning clear. In addition, both **quantity** and **product code** have been made optional as neither apply to OTHER ORDER LINE.

A **Type** column has been added to enable us to distinguish between the sub-types of ORDER LINE. A simple convention would be to use a code of 'POL' to mean PRODUCT ORDER LINE and 'OOL' to mean OTHER ORDER LINE – hence a three-character column.

Possible relational views, as defined in SQL, are as follows:

CREATE VIEW   OTHER_ORDER_LINES AS

SELECT   LINE_NUMBER,
                   ORDER_NUMBER,
                   DESCRIPTION,
                   TAX_COMMENT,
                   TYPE

FROM   ORDER_LINES
WHERE   TYPE = 'OOL'
WITH CHECK OPTION

CREATE VIEW   PRODUCT_ORDER_LINE AS

SELECT   LINE_NUMBER,
                   ORDER_NUMBER,
                   DESCRIPTION,
                   QUANTITY,
                   PRODUCT_CODE,
                   TYPE

FROM   ORDER_LINES
WHERE   TYPE = 'POL'
AND   QUANTITY NOT NULL
AND   EXISTS

(SELECT NULL FROM PRODUCTS WHERE
PRODUCTS.CODE = ORDER_LINES.PRODUCT_CODE)
WITH CHECK OPTION

Notice that both views check the **Type** column and the second view also enforces **not null** on quantity and ensures that there is a product code that matches an existing code from the PRODUCTS table.

Table for Sub-type

Tables are created for sub-types to cover all possible instances. Where there are many levels of sub-typing it is normal to use the first level down and create tables for all sub-types at that level. (Views could then be created for further sub-types.)

A table is created for the sub-type with candidate columns being created for each attribute and many to one relationship. On a similar basis, columns are created for its super-type (and so on up the hierarchy of sub-types) – each of these inherited columns maintains its optionality.

Where the sub-type is itself a super-type, optional candidate columns are also created for each of its sub-types (and so on down the hierarchy of sub-types).

A UNION view may also be created to enable you to process the super-type.

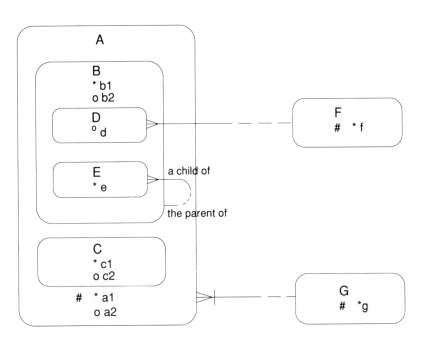

For the above example let us assume that a table is created for the sub-type B.

This is a complex example and is worthy of careful study as most of the circumstances that can be encountered are covered.

B		
b_1	not null	from sub-type B
b_2	null	
a_1	not null	
G_g	not null	primary key from super-type A
type	not null	
a_2	null	
d	null	from sub-type D and made optional
F_f	null	
e	null	from sub-type E
parent_a_1	null	from relationship between E and B,
parent_G_g	null	replicating primary key again for
parent_type	null	parent, then making them all
		optional

Let us also look at the view for sub-type E:

CREATE VIEW   E AS

SELECT   e,

b_1,

b_2,

a_1,

G_g,

type,

a_2,

parent_a_1,

parent_G_g,

parent_type

FROM   B
WHERE   type = 'E'
AND   e not null
AND   EXISTS

(SELECT NULL FROM B
WHERE $B \cdot a_1 = E \cdot Parent\_a_1$
AND $B \cdot G\_g = E \cdot parent\_G\_g$
AND $B \cdot Type = E \cdot Parent\_Type$)
WITH CHECK OPTION

And for completeness let us have a look at the UNION view for A.

CREATE VIEW   A AS

SELECT   * FROM B
UNION
SELECT   * FROM C

Note that the * above is a shorthand, which may be used with the ORACLE RDBMS to select all columns.

Advantages and
Disadvantages

All in one Table	Table for Sub-type
Advantages	Advantages
All in one place	Rules are more clearly aligned to the sub-types
Easy to access super-type and sub-types	Programs only work on tables that relate to the sub-types needed
Fewer tables needed	
Disadvantages	Disadvantages
Highly generic	Many extra tables
Logic needs to cater for different sets of columns and different integrity	Confusing columns on the UNION view
Potential bottleneck, particularly with some locking mechanisms	Potential performance issues on UNION view
Columns for sub-types must all be made optional	No updates are possible on the super-type, thus inhibiting functions that reference it.
On some RDBMS implementations you may run out of columns or take excessive space for null values.	

Step 7
Exclusive Relationship

There are two basic methods of handling the database design for use with exclusive relationships. These are:

– common domain
– explicit foreign keys.

Common domain

If the remaining foreign keys would all be in the same domain (identical format) then create two candidate columns:

– Relationship identifier
– Entity identifier.

The Relationship identifier column would be used to differentiate between the different relationships covered by the exclusive arc.

The Entity identifier column would be used to hold values for the unique identifier value of the entity at the far end of the appropriate relationship.

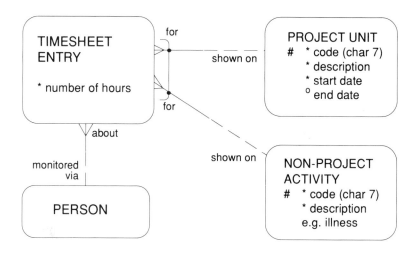

For the TIMESHEET_ENTRIES table, candidate columns to implement the relationships **for PROJECT UNIT** or **for NON-PROJECT ACTIVITY** would be:

Timesheet_for	char	3	not null	(value 'PU' and 'NPA')
Activity_code	char	7	not null	

Note that meaningful names have been chosen for both columns. **Activity_code** would take values for either PROJECT UNIT or NON-PROJECT ACTIVITY codes as appropriate. Both columns are **not null** for these mandatory relationships.

Explicit Foreign Keys

If the resulting foreign keys would not be in the same domain, create explicit foreign key columns for each relationship covered by the exclusive arc, and make all the resulting columns null (optional). Application code must now enforce the rule that only one may be entered, and that one **must** be entered if the relationships are mandatory.

Take the timesheet example again, but this time with the project unit code being an integer.

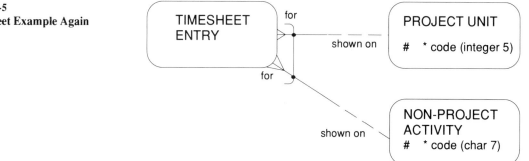

Resulting candidate columns are:

Project_units_code   integer   5   null
Non-project_activities_code   char   7   null

Advantages and
Disadvantages

Common Domain	Explicit Foreign Keys
Advantages	Advantages
Only two columns needed Optionality enforced by RDBMS	Join conditions are explicit
Disadvantages	Disadvantages
All joins must use both columns.	Excessive columns Optionality and usage must be enforced by the application.

Alternative Entity Models and their Impact on Design

The modelling conventions shown allow the same concepts to be modelled in several different ways. Let us have a look at three alternatives and how our design may be affected.

Figure F-6
Alternative 1

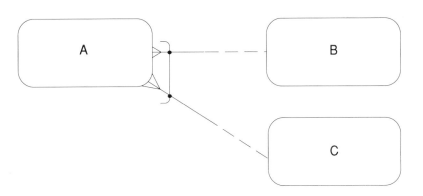

A simple exclusive arc, as covered earlier in this appendix.

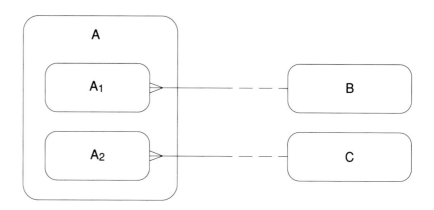

This is a much preferred model, as long as the sub-types A_1 and A_2 sensibly exist. Now the implementation of foreign keys does not need to worry about which 'parent' entity the relationship is pointing to.

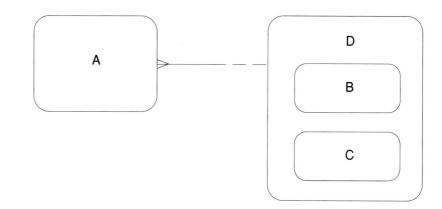

Once more this is preferred to Alternative 1, as the unique identifier of D can be used for both B and C. This model is, of course, only good if there is a sensible super-type, D.

Alternatives 2 and 3 both give us the opportunity to ask whether these concepts of A_1 and A_2 (with perhaps their own attributes/relationships or functions) and that of D (with its own attributes etc.) really exist.

Derived Attributes

Before we conclude this brief look at database design, it is sensible to look at the concept of derived attributes, which was mentioned before in Chapter 7.

The rule for database designers is that the value is derived only when needed. This would therefore break another rule – that attributes always become columns.

But what if the value of the attribute is repeatedly accessed by frequently-run programs and yet changes only rarely? It would be unnecessary to recalculate the value each time it is used if we create a column for the derived attribute, and have its value updated every time its source values change. The conditions for this alternative design are:

- the derived value changes rarely
- the cost of calculation is prohibitive. Normally this only occurs if the derivation involves more than one row on the database.

Next Steps

A large amount of the above default database design is carried out automatically, at your request, by leading CASE software.

But this is only a starting point, as the database design now needs careful scrutinizing to ensure that it provides full support in a performance/space efficient manner for the programs, ad hoc enquiries, archiving, and so on. This may require careful denormalization, controlled replication across a network, and detailed physical design of indexes and disk utilization.

Please ensure that you are familiar with such advanced database design techniques before starting a complex or critical design.

Appendix

G

BUSINESS VIEW

Business View

This is a concept which may be used to validate a model, help relate a model to existing systems and to simplify the definition of functions. It is also used to help define or visualize the interdependence of data when considering the problem of phased implementation of systems.

Definition

The business view of an entity is comprised of the attributes of the entity and the attributes of any other entities that are unambiguously related to it.

Or, to be more precise, the business view of an entity instance is made up of:

- the attributes of the subject entity, plus

- for any entity that the relationship definitions indicate that one and only one instance must be (or may be) related to the subject, then the attributes of these entity instances are also part of the business view, plus

- the attributes of other entities further removed, as identified by the above rule.

When an optional relationship or arc is used, all the attributes resulting from the corresponding relationship traversal (and subsequent ones) are considered optional. When different relationships target the same entity, the relationship name is used as a qualifier.

**Figure G-1
A Model Comprising
Simple Components**

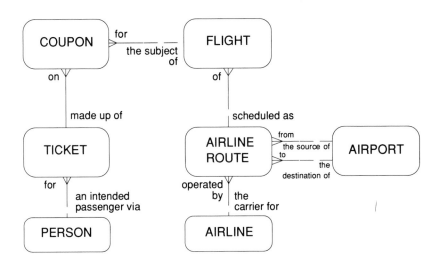

The business view of COUPON comprises:

COUPON (the subject entity)	class status confirmed indicator comment
FLIGHT	date of departure time of departure
AIRLINE ROUTE	flight number scheduled departure date
AIRLINE	code name
AIRPORT(from)	code name
AIRPORT (to)	code name
TICKET	date of issue fare currency
PERSON	name title initial

Notice that as there are two relationships between AIRLINE ROUTE and AIRPORT the relationship names have been used as qualifiers.

You will see how this 'flat file' view is very useful to cross-check against paper documents, file layouts, and so on.

The business view of FLIGHT is simply:

FLIGHT	date of departure
	time of departure
AIRLINE ROUTE	flight number
	scheduled departure time
AIRLINE	code
	name
AIRPORT(from)	code
	name
AIRPORT (to)	code
	name

Extended Business View

This becomes a little more complex when sub-types, recursive relationships and exclusive arcs are considered.

For recursive relationships, when the same attributes would be re-derived by going around the relationship again, insert '...'. When a relationship takes you to a sub-type, carry on from there as above and then start again from its super-type, and so on. When exclusive arcs are considered, go along each in turn.

A small real example with each is difficult to construct so the following illustrative example has been prepared.

Figure G-2
A Model Comprising More Complex Components

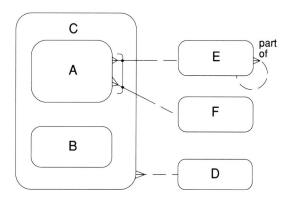

The business view of A for any instance of A is either:

A	a_1, a_2, a_3	(subject entity)
C	c_1, c_2, c_3	
D	d_1, d_2, d_3	(all optional)
F	f_1, f_2, f_3	

or:

A	a_1, a_2, a_3
C	c_1, c_2, c_3
D	d_1, d_2, d_3 (all optional)
E	e_1, e_2, e_3
E (part of)	$e_1, e_2, e_3 \ldots$ (all optional)

Notice that any real instance of an A type entity can have either E or F attributes, never both, as the relationships between entity A and entities E and F are mutually exclusive.

Named Business Views

It is often useful to have more than one business view from the same subject entity, where each one has a subset of the possible attributes. These subset business views may represent the information as normally perceived by part of the organization or from a functional viewpoint. Often, however, the names of the the attributes and their representation may normally be different from the compromise definitions we have agreed with our users. Further 'derived attributes' may be required to reflect the complete picture.

Let us take the same example we had at the beginning of this appendix and look at a couple of named subset business views.

Figure G-3

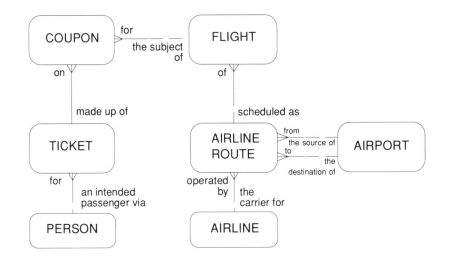

Remember the business view of FLIGHT was as follows:

FLIGHT   date of departure
                                    time of departure

AIRLINE ROUTE   flight number
                                    scheduled departure time

AIRLINE   code
                                    name

AIRPORT(from)   code
                                    name

AIRPORT (to)   code
                                    name

Notice again that as there are two alternative relationships between AIRLINE ROUTE and AIRPORT, the relationship names have been used as qualifiers.

We can now create a subset business view, which we will call REGULAR FLIGHT, which has the following data:

Figure G-4
Subset Business View

REGULAR FLIGHT	The Source		
	Entity	Attribute	Relationship
Date scheduled ← base attribute	Flight	date of departure	
Flight number ← changeable if transferable	Airline route	flight number	scheduled as
Departure time	Airline route	scheduled departure time	scheduled as
Airline	Airline	name	the carrier for
Destination	Airport (to)	name	the destination of
Origin	Airport (from)	name	the source of

descriptor

In this example we have omitted four attributes from the full business view and changed the names of several other attributes.

You will notice that the word **Airline** has been used as a simplification of Airline name – this use of the entity name or synonym is common and useful. The words **Destination** and **Origin** are role names, derived from the two relationship names between Airport and Airline Route – once more a common and useful technique.

We could now write definitions for business functions in terms of REGULAR FLIGHT and refer to these new definitions of information.

Example 1

Identify the flight number and date scheduled for any regular flight with an origin of 'Heathrow', where the date scheduled is during May 1989 and there is greater than one scheduled flight on the same date scheduled with an identical destination.

Example 2

A second example of a business function illustrates how a complex point of logic can often be handled in a very simple way by using a predefined business view.

Using the entity model directly gives the business definition:

*On demand, create an instance of a FLIGHT on a specified **date scheduled** of an AIRLINE ROUTE identified by a supplied **flight number** from an AIRPORT with a supplied **name** to an AIRPORT with a supplied **name**, run by an AIRLINE identified by a **code**, where the **name** of the AIRPORT that is the source of the AIRLINE ROUTE is not equal to the **name** of the AIRPORT that is the destination of the AIRLINE ROUTE.*

Using the REGULAR FLIGHT business view, this definition is simplified to:

*On demand, create an instance of a REGULAR FLIGHT using supplied **date scheduled, flight number, departure time, airline, destination and origin**, where the **destination** is not equal to the **origin***

In user terms this is much easier to understand, and the relationship links used in the original definition are completely implied when using the business view. The business view (and for that matter any entity definition) also implies the normal integrity constraints for attribute optionality and values. For example, if an attribute is mandatory and a date it is implicit that a value must be supplied and this value must be a valid date.

Thus the business definition could be simplified further to:

*On demand, create an instance of a REGULAR FLIGHT where the **destination** is not equal to the **origin**.*

When derived attributes have been defined, such as **number of coupons for flight** or **profit on ticket**, the logic still to be defined for a business function can often be reduced by another large factor.

Business Functions

So when defining functions it is useful to think in terms of business views. Simple functions tend to operate on a single business view, often of an intersection entity; for example, COUPON on a ticket for a flight. Other functions tend to operate on perhaps two or more business views, which then need to be correlated by reference to identical, derived attributes in their business views.

All the attributes in the business view could be used in the business function for **conditions where clauses** or to otherwise **identify** the target instances.

In general, only the attribute of the subject entity can be the subject of modification actions.

The only exception is when a modification attempts to change the attribute values that unambiguously correspond to the unique identifier of an entity that is directly related to the subject entity. This would represent an attempt to change the relationship.

For example, on the business view for COUPON, changing the flight number and date of departure would be an attempt to change the COUPON to enable you to catch a different FLIGHT.

For example, if a function worked on the REGULAR FLIGHT business view its attributes could be used as shown below.

Figure G-5
The Subset Business View
REGULAR FLIGHT

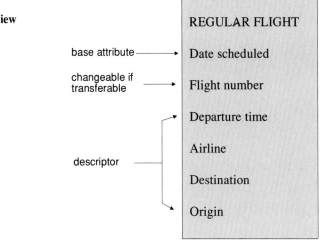

Data Dependence

At the end of a strategy study or during any subsequent stage of development it is useful to know what other data and related business functions must be implemented in a system to enable you to implement some really key item of data.

In our airline business, let us assume that the original paper system for knowing when flights were scheduled can no longer cope with the increase in air traffic we will computerize it very quickly. Subsequently, we will add details for tracking the tickets and coupons.

Figure G-6
The Extended Model
from Chapter 2

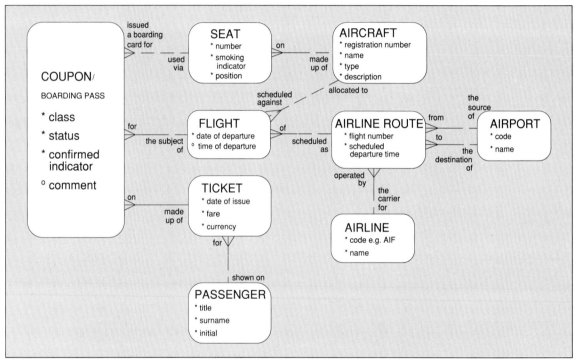

Data Dependence Rules

From the above diagram we can see that to implement details of FLIGHT we **must** also supply appropriate details of **AIRCRAFT AIRLINE ROUTE AIRLINE** and **AIRPORT**. This data dependence is easily identified if you look at the relationship definitions and obey the 'must be' rules; for example, FLIGHT must be of an AIRLINE ROUTE.

We also add in any entity that is unambiguously related to the subject entity by a many (or one) to one relationship; for example, FLIGHT may be allocated to an AIRCRAFT. In this case both mandatory and optional relationships are considered.

Details of entities further removed, as identified by the above two rules, must also be supplied.

Subsequently, to implement details of a TICKET, we must not only implement details of the PASSENGER but also that of COUPON, as a TICKET **must be** made up of one or more COUPONs. As a consequence, the rules of data dependence also enforce that we must add details that are implied by COUPON, which are those of:

> FLIGHT, AIRCRAFT (optional), AIRLINE ROUTE, AIRPORT (from), AIRPORT (to), AIRLINE, SEAT (optional) and AIRCRAFT (again for the seat (optional)).

This data dependence could be implied by simply looking at the full business view of COUPON.

Development Phases

You can then look at all the business functions that act upon these selected entities, or their business views, and select those that collectively make up sensible phases for development to meet the business needs, objectives and priorities.

This data dependence is reaffirmed by consideration of the important business views that need to be implemented.

Summary

Business views provide an elegant and powerful concept for communication with users in their terms, simplifying business function definitions and providing an insight into data dependence. The insight gained can then help with selection of implementation phasing, evaluation of alternative implementation techniques such as packages and with the identification of the likely data that must pass between two or more systems which must coexist.

Appendix

H   # META MODEL

What is a Meta Model?   A meta model, put simply, is a model of a model.

We have been modelling concepts such as credit card, account, flight, coupon and person.

A meta model would have diagrams and definitions covering the concepts of entity, attribute, domain, relationship and many of the other concepts mentioned in Chapter 9 and in the Glossary of Terms. The simple diagram below covers the main concepts covered in this book.

Figure H-1
Simple Meta Model

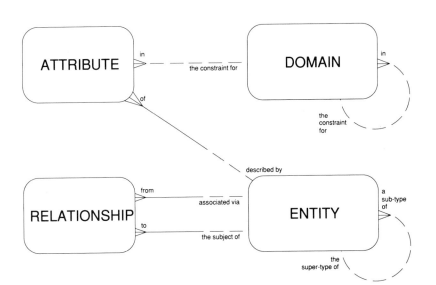

Reading Meta Models

Meta models can be validated and read in the same way as ordinary models, for example:

Each ENTITY may be a sub-type of one and only one other ENTITY and it may also be a super-type of two or more other ENTITIES.

It may be described by one or more ATTRIBUTES, each of which may be in one and only one DOMAIN.

In addition, each ENTITY may be associated via one or many RELATIONSHIPS, each of which is to another of the same ENTITY.

The following model covers most of the meta concepts covered in this book.

Figure H-2
Meta Model of the Concepts
Covered in this Book

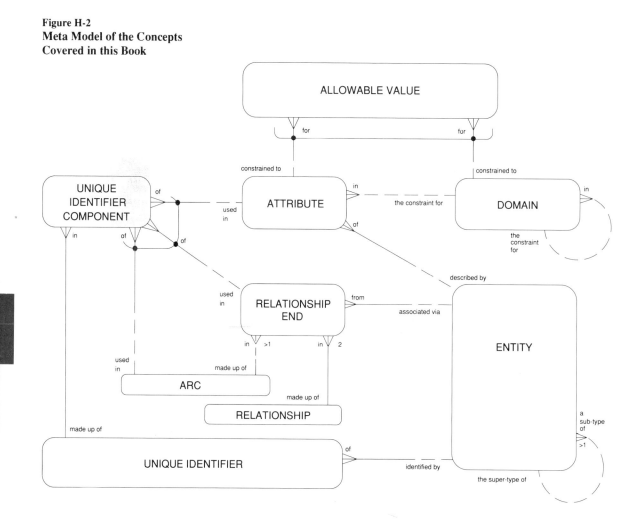

Appendix

I

ATLANTIS ISLAND FLIGHTS – FULL MODEL

This appendix contains an entity relationship model for Atlantis Island Flights produced by Oracle's CASE*Designer software product. A small subset of the full model is shown on page 2 as it appears on the screen of the Entity Relationship Diagrammer from the CASE*Designer product.

As you may have gathered the airline is a make-believe one, and the model is thus not only definitive but contains many omissions and differences when compared with a real airline. Why not spend some time checking out some area of detail not covered by the notes and learn from that enquiring procedure?

A print from the CASE*Dictionary software product has also been included for a few of the entities defined.

See page 3   for   TICKET
      page 4   COUPON
      pages 5-6   AIRLINE ROUTE
      page 7   CREW ASSIGNMENT

**Example Entity
Relationship Diagrammer**

Many CASE vendors supply Entity Relationship Diagrammers in their product set. The one shown is from CASE*Designer, a multi-windowed, multi-user workstation product from Oracle Corporation.

A useful facility with such a tool is the ability to select an entity and then resize, move and stretch it over other entities (i.e. make sub-types), and generally optimize the diagram layout. The menu options can be used to add attribute details, perform default database design and to support many of the other activities of strategists, analysts and database designers. Similar diagrammers are available for other techniques, such as Dataflow modelling, Matrix handling, Function Hierarchies, etc.

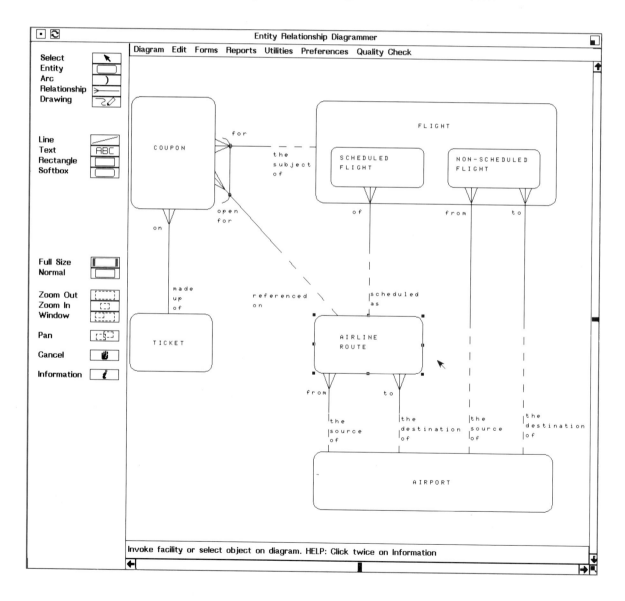

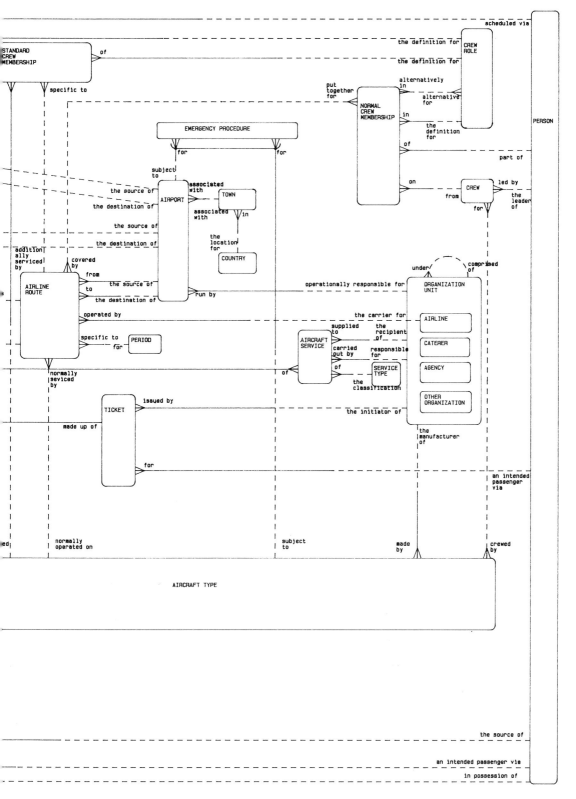

```
Date : 01-AUG-89          ORACLE : CASE*Dictionary        Page :         1
                       DETAILED ENTITY DEFINITION

Entity Name : TICKET                      Application :        ATBS
                                          Version     :           1

Sub-type of :                             Reference   :      TICKET

Synonyms    : GROUP TICKET                Initial Volume :
                                          Average Volume :    60000
                                          Maximum Volume :
                                          Annual Growth% :       15


--- DESCRIPTION - HAS SIGNIFICANCE AS -------------------------------------

A means of acquiring the right to fly with an airline as a passenger.
#
A contractual document between an airline and a person, which may be
exchanged, cashed in, or its constituent coupons exchanged for
a journey with  this or another airline.


--- ATTRIBUTES ------------------------------------------------------------

Name : CURRENCY                        Domain : CHAR CODE
       Opt : N         Format : CHAR   Length : 3
Name : DATE OF ISSUE                   Domain :
       Opt : N         Format : DATE   Length :
Name : DISCOUNT GIVEN                  Domain :
       Opt : N         Format : MONEY  Length : 6,2
Name : FULL FARE                       Domain :
       Opt : N         Format : MONEY  Length : 6,2
Name : NUMBER                          Domain :
       Opt : N         Format    :     Length : 9                *
                       INTEGER
Name : STAFF INDICATOR                 Domain :
       Opt : N         Format : CHAR   Length : 1
Name : TIME OF ISSUE                   Domain :
       Opt : N         Format : TIME   Length :

                          * - Attributes in primary unique identifier

--- RELATIONSHIPS ---------------------------------------------------------

EACH OCCURRENCE OF THIS ENTITY :

MUST BE made up of          ONE OR MORE    COUPONS
MUST BE issued by       ONE AND ONLY ONE   ORGANIZATION UNIT
MUST BE for             ONE AND ONLY ONE   PERSON

                   * - Relationships in primary unique identifier

--- NOTES AND REMARKS -----------------------------------------------------
```

DETAILED ENTITY DEFINITION

Entity Name : COUPON   Application :   ATBS
                                               Version   :   1

Sub-type of :   Reference   :   COUPON

Synonyms   :   Initial Volume :
                                               Average Volume :   90000
                                               Maximum Volume :
                                               Annual Growth% :

--- DESCRIPTION - HAS SIGNIFICANCE AS ------------------------------------

That part of a ticket which entitles the named passenger to travel on
a specified flight of an aircraft, assuming there is an available
seat.
The passenger would normally have an (implicitly) associated booking
and subsequent boarding pass for the same flight.

--- ATTRIBUTES ---

Name : CHECK-IN TIME   Domain :
       Opt : Y   Format : TIME   Length : 4
Name : COMMENT   Domain :
       Opt : Y   Format : CHAR   Length : 20
Name : CONFIRMED INDICATOR   Domain : INDICATOR
       Opt : Y   Format : CHAR   Length : 1
Name : FINAL CHECK-IN TIME   Domain :
       Opt : Y   Format : TIME   Length : 4
Name : STATUS   Domain :
       Opt : Y   Format : CHAR   Length : 1

                        * - Attributes in primary unique identifier

--- RELATIONSHIPS --

EACH OCCURRENCE OF THIS ENTITY :

MUST BE for   ONE AND ONLY ONE   SEAT CLASS
MUST BE on   ONE AND ONLY ONE   TICKET   *

MUST BE open for   ONE AND ONLY ONE   AIRLINE ROUTE   *
OR
MUST BE for   ONE AND ONLY ONE   FLIGHT   *

                  * - Relationships in primary unique identifier

--- NOTES AND REMARKS --

DETAILED ENTITY DEFINITION

Entity Name : AIRLINE ROUTE   Application :   ATBS
                                               Version   :   1

Sub-type of :   Reference   :   ROUTE

Synonyms   :   Initial Volume :
                                               Average Volume :   50
                                               Maximum Volume :
                                               Annual Growth% :   5

--- DESCRIPTION - HAS SIGNIFICANCE AS -------------------------------------

A standard route flown by an airline on an approved schedule.

--- ATTRIBUTES --

Name : BOOKABLE SEATS INDICATOR   Domain : INDICATOR
     Opt : N   Format : CHAR   Length : 1
Name : FLIGHT NUMBER   Domain :
     Opt : N   Format : CHAR   Length : 6   *
Name : STANDARD FARE   Domain :
     Opt : N   Format : MONEY   Length : 6.2
Name : STANDARD FARE CURRENCY   Domain : CHAR CODE
     Opt : N   Format : CHAR   Length : 3
Name : DEPARTURE DAY   Domain :
     Opt : Y   Format : CHAR   Length : 12
Name : REFRESHMENT TYPE   Domain : CHAR CODE
     Opt : Y   Format : CHAR   Length : 3
Name : SCHEDULED ARRIVAL TIME   Domain :
     Opt : Y   Format : TIME   Length : 4
Name : SCHEDULED DEPARTURE TIME   Domain :
     Opt : Y   Format : TIME   Length : 4

                         * - Attributes in primary unique identifier

--- RELATIONSHIPS ---

EACH OCCURRENCE OF THIS ENTITY :

MUST BE operated by   ONE AND ONLY ONE AIRLINE   *
MUST BE to   ONE AND ONLY ONE AIRPORT
MUST BE from   ONE AND ONLY ONE AIRPORT
MUST BE specific to   ONE AND ONLY ONE PERIOD
MAY BE normally serviced by ONE AND ONLY ONE AIRCRAFT TYPE
MAY BE referenced on   ONE OR MORE   COUPONS

Entity Name : AIRLINE ROUTE   Application :   ATBS
                                               Version   :   1
Sub-type of :   Reference   :   ROUTE

--- RELATIONSHIPS --
EACH OCCURRENCE OF THIS ENTITY :

MAY BE   covered by   ONE OR MORE   NORMAL CREW MEMBERSHIPS
MAY BE   scheduled as   ONE OR MORE   SCHEDULED FLIGHTS
MAY BE   additionally serviced ONE OR MORE   STANDARD   CREW
         by   MEMBERSHIPS

                        * - Relationships in primary unique identifier
--- NOTES AND REMARKS --

DETAILED ENTITY DEFINITION

Entity Name : CREW ASSIGNMENT   Application :   ATBS
                                                 Version   :   1

Sub-type of :   Reference   :   CREW ASSIG

Synonyms   :   Initial Volume :
                                                 Average Volume :   85000
                                                 Maximum Volume :
                                                 Annual Growth% :

--- DESCRIPTION - HAS SIGNIFICANCE AS ------------------------------------

An allocation of a person, who must be an existing member of a crew,
to either a complete flight or a component of a flight. Each assignment is within the context of a specific crew role, which may differ
from their normal crew role. Eg A captain acting as a second pilot.

--- ATTRIBUTES ---

Name : DATE CANCELLED   Domain :
       Opt : Y   Format : DATE   Length :
Name : DATE MADE   Domain :
       Opt : Y   Format : DATE   Length :
Name : SPECIAL DUTY   Domain :
       Opt : Y   Format : CHAR   Length : 80

                         * - Attributes in primary unique identifier

--- RELATIONSHIPS --

EACH OCCURRENCE OF THIS ENTITY :

MUST BE in   ONE AND ONLY ONE   CREW ROLE
MUST BE of   ONE AND ONLY ONE   PERSON   *

MUST BE to   ONE AND ONLY ONE   FLIGHT   *
OR
MUST BE to   ONE AND ONLY ONE   FLIGHT COMPONENT   *

                     * - Relationships in primary unique identifier

--- NOTES AND REMARKS --

Appendix

J

OTHER MODELLING CONVENTIONS

Entity relationship modelling is a technique which is used in most development methodologies; however, the concepts encompassed by the technique are often represented diagrammatically in different ways. It is not possible within the scope of this book to cover all of the alternative representations, but a few have been included as illustrations.

The following diagram is shown initially using the method outlined in this book and then by alternative methods.

Figure J-1
A Model of an Order and its Order Lines Using the CASE*Method Conventions

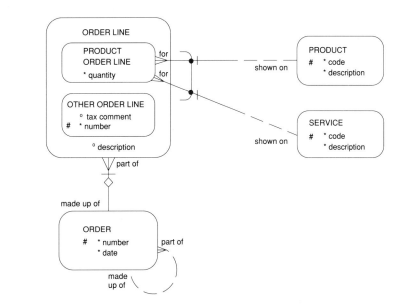

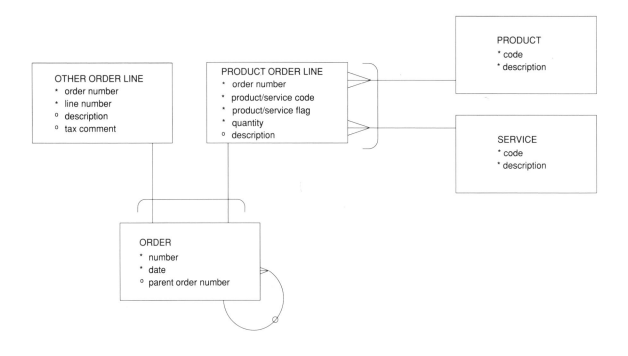

You will note that the one to many relationships are similar, as is the use of the exclusive arc. At this time sub-types, unique identifiers and non-transferable relationships are not generally shown. Here the sub-types have been modelléd by the use of an exclusive arc from ORDER.

Role attributes are used to indicate how the relationship is to be modelled; for example, on the entity PRODUCT ORDER LINE the order number is replicated to indicate the relationship to an ORDER.

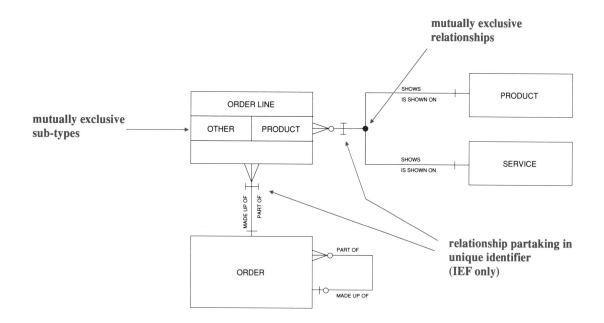

Notice the optional indicator ——○—— on the relationship is at the opposite end to that shown in CASE*Method. The ——+—— symbol shows the **one** end of a relationship.

CASE*Method is in essence a methodology that would be categorized as information engineering, as a consequence of which most of the entity relationship modelling concepts are covered, using different conventions as shown.

Chen Model

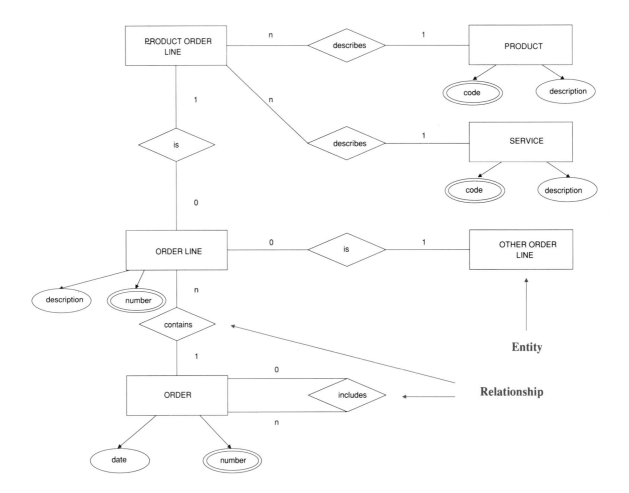

Although it is not illustrated in the above diagram, relationships are not constrained to only having two ends (binary relationships). In Chen entity modelling, as in the Merise method, a relationship may be between two, three or more entities and in addition a relationship may have attributes of its own.

Attributes are shown in ellipses attached to the relevant entity or relationship and Unique Identifiers of entities are indicated by a double ellipse. Only some of the attributes are shown on this diagram to avoid congestion. Sub-types are shown by one to one binary relationships, exclusivity and non-transferability of relationships are not generally shown.

GLOSSARY OF TERMS

This glossary contains a list of terms used in the CASE*Method references and associated documents. Some of the words may not appear in this particular document, but they are included here for your information.

You will also find that a few dictionary definitions have been added to illustrate the definitive meaning of a word in **current** English usage. These have been taken from *The Concise Oxford Dictionary of Current English 8th edition,* © *1990 Oxford University Press.*

Access Control　　The ability to manage which users or groups of users may have the privilege to retrieve, create, update or delete data that is held in a database. Access may be granted or revoked by the owner of the data.

Activity　　Anything that needs to be done to complete a task.

Aim　　See **Business Aim**.

ANSI　　American National Standards Institute.

Application System　　A name given to an arbitrary collection of business functions, entities, programs and tables.

Arc　　A means of identifying two or more mutually exclusive relationships. See **Exclusive Arc**.

Attribute　　Any detail that serves to qualify, identify, classify, quantify or express the state of an entity.

or
Any description of 'a thing of significance'.

Note that each entity occurrence may only have one value of any attribute at one time.

attribute *n.*　　**1 a**　a quality ascribed to a person or thing. **b**　a characteristic quality. **2**　a material object recognized as appropriate to person, office, or status (*a large car is an attribute of seniority*) ...

Business Aim　　A statement of business intent that may be measured subjectively; for example, to move up-market or to develop a sustainable level of growth.

Business Constraint　　Any external, management or other factor that may confine the business or development in terms of resource availability, dependencies or timescales.

Business Function　　What a business does or needs to do, irrespective of how it does it. See **Elementary Business Function**.

Business Location   A uniquely identifiable geographic location, from which one or more business units may be wholly or partially operating.

Business Model   See **Entity Relationship Diagram** and **Function Hierarchy**.

Business Objective   A statement of business intent that may be measured quantifiably.

Aims and objectives are similar concepts but the achievement of an objective is measurable in some specific manner; for example, to increase profit by 1% during the next financial year.

Business Performance Indicator   Any measure that may be used to quantify the success or failure of a business objective.

Business Priority   A statement of important business need or requirement within an ordered list.

Business System Life Cycle   The structured approach used in CASE*Method for the task of developing a business system. The seven major stages are strategy, analysis, design, build, documentation, transition and production. (Also called the development life-cycle.)

Business Unit   Part of an organization which is treated for any purpose as a separate formation within the parent organization; for example, a department.

CASE   Computer-Aided Systems Engineering is the combination of graphical, dictionary, generator, project management and other software tools to assist computer development staff engineer and maintain high-quality systems for their end users, within the framework of a structured method.

CASE*Designer   CASE*Designer is a work-station-based development environment, designed for use by system engineers such as analysts and designers. It provides a multi-windowed, multi-user, networked access to many development tools, in particular CASE*Dictionary. It also provides a set of interactive diagrammers and plotting facilities to enable concepts, such as entity relationship models, to be manipulated and output graphically. It is fully integrated with CASE*Dictionary.

CASE*Dictionary   A database or repository for system development staff to record all significant

results from the strategy, analysis, design and implementation stages of the system development.

CASE*Method   CASE*Method is a structured approach to engineering systems in a data processing environment. It consists of a set of stages, tasks, deliverables and techniques, which lead you through all steps in the life-cycle of a system. It is delivered to you via training courses, books and consultancy support, and can be automated by a wide range of CASE tools from both Oracle and other companies.

Character   A single location on the computer system capable of holding one alphabetic character or numeric digit. One or more characters are held in a field. One or more fields comprise a record, and one or more records may be held in a file.
or
The format of an attribute, which may contain alphabetic characters or numeric digits.

Column   A means of implementing an item of data within a table. It can be in character, date or number format, and be optional or mandatory.
or
An implementation of an attribute or relationship.

Common Function   During analysis, the objective is to eliminate identical functions wherever possible by overlapping, making them more generic or recognizing that they were not identical in the first place. When this is not practical, one or more common functions may be created, each of which is a slave to (copy of) a master function. Only the master function may then be further described, whilst the slave functions can appear in different parts of the function hierarchy, as required.

Critical Success Factor   Any business event, dependency, deliverable or other factor which, if not attained, would seriously impair the likelihood of achieving a business objective.

Database   An arbitrary collection of tables or files under the control of a database management system.

Data Dictionary   A database for holding definitions of tables, columns and views, and so on. See also **CASE*Dictionary.**

Dataflow   A named flow of data between business functions, datastores and external entities. See **Business Function**, **Datastore** and **External Entity**.

Data Item   In some systems the definition of a logical data item is equivalent to an attribute at the business level. When used with other file management systems, a data item is a means of implementing an item of data within a file.

The term data item is sometimes used as an equivalent to column. See **Attribute** or **Column.**

Datastore   A temporary or permanent storage concept for logical data items/attributes, as used by specified business functions/processes.

DBMS   A database management system, normally encompassing computerized management facilities that are used to structure and manipulate data, and to ensure privacy, recovery and integrity in a multi-user environment.

Derived Data Item   A value that is derived by some algorithm from the values of other data items; for example, profit, which is the difference between income and costs.

Development Life-cycle   See **Business System Life Cycle**.

Distributed Database   A database that is physically located on more than one computer processor, connected via some form of communications network. An essential feature of a true distributed database is that the user and/or program work as if they had access to the whole database locally. All processing to give this impression is carried out by the database management system.

Distributed Processing   The ability to have several computers working together in a distributed network, where each processor can be used to run different activities for a user, as required.

Domain   A set of business validation rules, format constraints and other properties that apply to a group of attributes. For example:

- a list of values
- a range
- a qualified list or range
- any combination of these.

Note that attributes and columns in the same domain are subject to a common set of validation checks.

Elementary Business Function   A business function which, if started, must be completed. It cannot exist in an intermediate stage. Elementary business functions are at the lowest level of a function hierarchy and cannot be further decomposed. See **Function Hierarchy**.

Entity   A thing of significance, whether real or imagined, about which information needs to be known or held. See **Attribute**.

entity *n.*   **1**   a thing with distinct existence, as opposed to a quality or relation ...

Entity Relationship Diagram   A part of the business model produced in the strategy stage of the Business System Life Cycle. The diagram pictorially represents entities, the vital business relationships between them and the attributes used to describe them. See **Entity, Attribute**, **Relationship** and **Entity Relationship Diagrammer**.

The process of creating this diagram is called entity relationship modelling. The terms entity model, entity relationship model and entity/relationship model are all synonyms for Entity Relationship Diagram.

Entity Relationship Diagrammer   A CASE tool that enables you to interactively draw and change complete (or subset) Entity Relationship Diagrams; it should be possible to produce and amend diagrams and to update the CASE dictionary itself via the diagrams within the context of a specific version of an application system.

Event   There are three types of event, all of which may act as triggers to one or more business functions.

External or Change Event – any point in the life of the enterprise when, under specified conditions, data is created or changed in such a manner as to act as a trigger for some business function(s). It may be identified when an entity is created or deleted, the value of an attribute is changed, or a relationship is connected or disconnected.

Realtime Event – any point in the life of an enterprise when, under specified conditions, real time reaches a predetermined date and time.

System Event – any point in the life of an enterprise when one or more functions have been completed, which event acts as a trigger to initiate further functions.

Exclusive Arc   Two or more relationships are diagrammatically shown to be mutually exclusive by means of an exclusive arc. See **Arc**.

External Business Function   A business function, outside the scope of the application system, that acts as a source or recipient of dataflows into or out of the system.

External Entity   A thing of significance, outside the scope of the application system, that acts as a source or recipient of dataflows into or out of the system.

Field   A means of implementing an item of data within a file. It can be in character, date, number or other format, and be optional or mandatory.

File   A method of implementing part or all of a database.

Foreign Key   One or more columns in a table that implement a many to one relationship that the table in question has with another table. This concept allows the two tables to be joined together.

Format   The type of data that an attribute or column may represent; for example, character, date, number.

Function   See **Business** and **Elementary Business Function.**

Function Decomposition   Any business function may be decomposed into lower levels of detail that are business functions themselves, and so on, until reaching the business functions that are elementary. This function decomposition gives rise to functions arranged in groups/hierarchies known as a business function hierarchy.

Function Hierarchy   A simple grouping of functions in a strict hierarchy, representing all the functions in an area of a business. This forms part of the business model produced in the strategy stage of the Business System Life Cycle. See **Business Function**.

Index   A means of accessing one or more rows in a table with particular performance characteristics, often implemented by a B-tree structure on an RDBMS. An index may quote one or more columns and be a means of enforcing uniqueness on their values.

Key   Any set of columns that is frequently used for retrieval of rows from a table. See also **Unique Identifier** and **Column**.

Location   See **Business Location**.

Matrix Diagrammer   A CASE tool that enables you to create and change complete (or subset) matrices interactively. Matrices covered include:

- Function: Entity
- Function: Business Unit
- Function: Module
- Entity: Business Unit
- Entity: Table
- Module: Table
- Module: Module.

Mouse   A pointing device, attached to a workstation, which can be used to pass x, y co-ordinates to a program via its pointing facilities. A mouse will normally have between one and three buttons, which may also signify different things when clicked.

Normalization   A step-by-step process that produces either entity or table definitions that have:

- no repeating groups
- the same kind of values assigned to attributes or columns
- a distinct name
- distinct and uniquely identifiable rows.

Null   A column, field or data item may, in some implementations be required to reserve a value that means 'there is no current value' – this is known as a null value. Other implementations, such as the ORACLE RDBMS (and paper!), implement this concept correctly, by having 'no value' to signify there is no current value.

Operation   In other methodologies the term operation has the same meaning as business function or elementary business function when used in a business context. See **Business Function** and **Elementary Business Function.**

Primary Index   An index used to improve performance on the combination of columns most frequently used to access rows in a table.

Primary Key   The set of mandatory columns within a table that is used to enforce uniqueness of rows, and that is normally the most frequent means by which rows are accessed.

Process   In other methodologies the term process has the same meaning as business function or elementary business function when used in a business context. See **Business Function** and **Elementary Business Function**.

Program   A set of computer instructions, which can enter, change or query database items, and provide many useful computer functions.

RDBMS   Relational database management system.

Record   In a non-relational database system, a record is an entry in a file, consisting of individual elements of information, which together provide full details about an aspect of the information needed by the system. The individual elements are held in fields, and all records are held in files. An example of a record might be an employee. Every detail of the employee (e.g. date of birth, department code, full names) will be found in a number of fields.

In a relational system record is an alternative word for row. See **Row**.

Record Type   A predetermined set of fields within a file.

Relation   A relation is a term that embraces the concepts of both table and view. See **Table** and **View**.

relation *n.*   **1 a** what one person or thing has to do with another. **b** the way in which one person stands or is related to another. **c** the existence or effect of a connection, correspondence, contrast, or feeling prevailing between persons or things, esp. when qualified in some way ...

Relationship   What one thing has to do with another.
or
Any significant way in which two things of the same or different type may be associated.

Note that it is important to name relationships.

Row   An entry in a table, consisting of values for each relevant column.

Schema   A collection of table definitions.

SQL   Structured Query Language. The internationally-accepted standard for relational systems, covering not only query but also data definition, manipulation, security and some aspects of referential integrity.

Stage   One of the seven major parts of the CASE*Method Business System Life Cycle.

Sub-entity   Synonymous with sub-type. See **Sub-type.**

Sub-schema   A subset of a schema. In relational terms, a view is often a more applicable concept.

Sub-type   A type of entity. An entity may be split into two or more sub-types, each of which has common attributes and/or relationships. These are defined explicitly once only at the higher level. Sub-types may have attributes and/or relationships in their own right. A sub-type may be further sub-typed to lower levels.

Super-type   A means of classifying an entity that has sub-types.

System   See **Application System**.

Table   A tabular view of data, which may be used on a relational database management system to hold one or more columns of data. It is often an implementation of an entity. Tables are the logical and perceived data structure, not the physical data structure, in a relational system.

thing *n.*   **1** a material or non-material entity, idea, action, etc., that is or may be thought about or perceived. **2** an inanimate material object (*take that thing away*). **3** an unspecified object or item (*have a few things to buy*) ... **6** a quality (*patience is a useful thing*) ... **8** a specimen or type of something (*the latest thing in hats*) ...

Unique Identifier   Any combination of attributes and/or relationships that serves, in all cases, to uniquely identify an occurrence of an entity.
or
One or more columns that will always supply a single row from a table.

Version Control   A mechanism to help system engineers handle the problem of a system going into a production (live) state and then moving on to a second or subsequent development state. Version control is a facility that includes the capability of changing the state of a version of an application, archiving a version, creating new versions, and so on.

View   A means of accessing a subset of the database as if it were a table. The view may:

- be restricted to named columns
- be restricted to specific rows
- change column names
- derive new columns
- give access to a combination of related tables and/or views.

INDEX

D